5th Edition

INSPIRING ENTREPRENEURS

JOURNEY FROM 'CAN I' to 'I CAN!'

Compiled and Authored by

Anju Handa

ISBN
Paperback: 979-8-89067-626-9
Hardcase: 979-8-89067-926-0

Dedication

I dedicate 5th edition of my book INSPIRING ENTREPRENEURS ....JOURNEY FROM CAN I TO I CAN to my loving parents LATE SH. VED PRAKASH ANAND AND SMT. SHAKUNTALA ANAND who always remained a source of inspiration to me for all my endevours and success. I owe my life to them and want every child to hold their parents fingers when they are old, like they hold their children when hey are small.

Contents

Foreword 7

Preface 9

1. **Captain Mayuri Deshmukh** 11
   Helicopter pilot, Indias first woman offshore captain

2. **Dr. Kuiljeit Uppaal** 17
   Worlds First Image Scientist Impact Strategist & CEO-KREA

3. **Consulate Syed Algazi** 25
   His Excellency Nawab Syed Algazi, Honorary Consul of the Republic of Liberland (Europe),
   Chairman and Managing Director, N.F. Constructions India-Dubai, Founder &
   Chairperson, Braveheart MARTYRS Foundation

4. **Neelam Berry** 37
   Managing Director Cistula Tulip Films Writer and Producer of Films

5. **Hema Paul** 43
   Founder & MD Femvings

6. **Rajni Gobhil** 49
   Founder Meri Pehchan Me

7. **Gurleen Khokhar** 59
   Internationally Renowned Mental Health Expert CEO Dhun App Transformational
   Speaker Chairperson International Human Rights NGO, Director NCNB, Author Model,
   Former Principal

8. Sanjay Kumar Agarwal **69**

Mentor, and coach Gopala NLP Master Trainer, Growth Accelerator Coach, TEDx Speaker & Author

9. Aditi Handa **77**

Co Founder & Head Chef the Bakers Dozen

10. Jaiparkash Sharma **89**

Differently Abled Social Activist, Motivational Speaker Certified Changemaker By Govt of India, Prop. Dadhich Stone & Deedwania Udhyog RIICO

11. Gayatri Chadwa **97**

Founder SVA Eternal, Maharashtra State Chair, G100 Diversity & Inclusion Wing

12. Neelam Khemka **105**

Poetess & Social Worker

Foreword

Foreword

With a current proportion of 48.4%, the female population in India stands poised at the cusp of progress, while men make up 51.6% of the population. Women wield significant potential in driving the nation's economic growth. Despite strides, Indian women continue to challenge the barriers of patriarchy and gender disparity. Ensuring the inclusion of women becomes a paramount consideration, particularly in the context of the Indian job market.

Over the course of history, women have endured the weight of societal injustices and biases. However, in this era of evolving perspectives, hey have managed to carve out a distinct identity. Casting aside the constraints of traditional gender norms, they have risen above and pursued their aspirations with unwavering determination. Some inspiring examples are Sindhutai Sapkal Social activist, Mary Kom, PV Sindhu and of course our very own Indian Women's cricket team.

The forefront of various governmental efforts has been dedicated to fostering women's empowerment, resulting in a series of transformative amendments within the Indian Constitution. The doctrine of gender parity is deeply ingrained within the Indian Constitution, spanning across its Preamble, Fundamental Rights, Fundamental Duties, and Directive Principles. This embodiment extends beyond mere equality, extending the State's authority to implement affirmative actions favoring women. These measures are designed to counterbalance the enduring socio-economic, educational, and political disparities women have confronted over centuries.

Anju Handa has imparted to us narratives depicting the journeys of noteworthy individuals, both men and women, outlining their challenges and eventually their paths to victory. These individuals stand as true examples of accomplishment. The 5th edition of the book Inspiring Entrepreneurs – A Journey from Can I to I Can" is poised to impart a potent message to a wide audience, potentially shaping the direction of societal transformation.

Sandeep Marwah
Chancellor

AAFT UNIVERSITY OF MEDIA AND ARTS: Maath, Kharora, Distt. Raipur-493225, Chhattisgarh, India
Tel: +91 91110-11744 | www.aaft.edu.in | support@aaft.edu.in

Preface

"You may not control all the events that happen to you, but you can decide not to be reduced by them"

Maya Angelou – Poet

Dear Friends,

It gives me great pleasure to present the fourth edition of the book chronicling, the struggle and achievement of 3 men and 9 women entrepreneur, who had the courage and audacity to swim against the current and affixed their stamp of individuality and authority in the highly polarised society. The way they balanced their diverse responsibilities and emerged shining against all odds is tribute to their leadership. The simple tale of success as elucidated in these pages is fascinating and motivating, and in all probability will go a long way towards our solemn initiative of women empowerment. It's our firm belief and conviction that gender equality is not only a fundamental right, but necessary foundation for a peaceful, prosperous and sustainable world.

There has been progress over the last decades: More girls are going to school, fewer girls are forced into early marriages, more women are serving in parliament and positions of leadership, and laws are being reformed to advance gender inequality. However, while cherishing the euphoria, let us not dilute our vision and guard against any type of complacency sweeping in eroding our sacrosanct vision and values. Despite this gain many challenges remain: discriminatory laws and social norms remain pervasive, women continue to be underrepresented at all levels of political leadership.

It's just a beginning and still long way to go to achieve the equilibrium in this lopsided, discriminatory world wherein, we are still highly marginalised. We are better off today, but far from equal with men. Adorned with patience and perseverance we will attain the pinnacle of success. Let us consciously work towards Social Empowerment, Economic empowerment and political Empowerment, the tripod on which our vision and aspirations will find its fulfilment.

Education, self-reliance, character, simplicity, decent behaviour and awareness will instrumental in culminating eradication of this imbalance as asserted in last edition. Further, we should enhance our umbrella to bring all class of women into our ambit, guarding that the vision and dreams does not limit itself to erudite class and remain confine to meeting and associations in air condition rooms and hotels.

The gender bias may be a global phenomenon, but it becomes more pronounced in Indian context, which has its genesis in cultural heritage of our nation which though great was perverted to narrow parochial aims of self-aggrandisement. The problems of women living in slums and socio economic oppression of the working class and peasant women have always been to the forefront. This is hardly surprising, as the overwhelming majority of women in India live in conditions of extreme poverty and deprivation. At the same time, rape, wife beating, economically motivated killings and other atrocities against women show no sign of declining. The task confronting the women's empowerment in India are formidable indeed.

Friends, we need to shed our urban goggles, step down to integrate all class women lending a helping hand towards our comprehensive goal. Little words of comfort and understanding will transcend their confidence to achievement levels, trespassing the educational lacunae and motivating them in raising their voices against the discrimination creating a new eco system of egalitarian society.

Let us applause the motivation of young men and women, lending our helping hand and support towards a neo ecosystem. Signing off with the immortal words of Robert Frost.

I have promises to keep.
...... and miles to go before I sleep,
miles to go before I sleep.

CAPTAIN MAYURI DESHMUKH

Captain Mayuri Deshmukh

Helicopter pilot,
Indias first woman offshore captain

Her unwavering dedication and exceptional skills have made this journey of hers an inspiring story for young women to pursue a career in helicopters as well.

On International Women's Day 2022, Capt Mayuri Deshmukh, a commercial helicopter pilot, became India's first woman offshore captain. She has been awarded by the Ministry of Civil Aviation and Rotary Wing Society of India for Excellence in the field of Aviation. She also holds a record with 'Limca Book of Records' for her offshore qualification.

Who is she?

Daughter of a retired Indian Air Force officer, she took to flying helicopters as a passion after watching her father fly helicopters into the remotest areas of India. Listening to the exhilarating tales of flying this complex machine and watching him take off and land across the runways made her resolve stronger to become a Rotary Wing pilot. She went for flying training after completing her Mass Communications degree from Xavier's Institute Mumbai to the United States in 2008 after doing

a lot of research for flying schools since there were no training schools in India. Her sister is also a commercial pilot flying Airbus 320 with a reputed airline in India making it a trio of pilots in the family.

Career Path

From the first job which started in 2008 as a dispatcher and coordinator for a company, her first flying break came with flying for Reliance Industries Ltd on Dauphin N3 helicopters. Her job there was mainly to fly high-level directors and VIPs, which was a great exposure towards corporate flying. After gaining some experience as a co-pilot, she moved on to join India's largest helicopter company, Pawan Hans Ltd., which gave her the chance to explore the unexplored. She gained experience by flying pan India, through hills, seas, and Naxal areas, sunrise to sunset, ferrying helicopters to the most unexplored and remote terrains of the Northern plains and carrying out medical evacuations over the Islands of Lakshadweep and Port Blair. She has flown actively in the rescue of COVID-positive patients to the mainland.

However, though the company had a lot of onshore flying detachments, what caught

Movies 17
Amitabh Bachchan says Aamir Khan got 'over-excited' after watching 'Jhund'

City boasts India's first woman pilot to lead offshore flight

Flying over Bombay High in a helicopter was the most beautiful experience, says Captain Mayuri Deshmukh

Manju V
mirrorfeedback@timesgroup.com

TWEETS @MumbaiMirror

Hundreds of civil aviation aircraft take off from Mumbai daily, many head west to overfly the Arabian sea and inside quite a few of these cockpits would be women pilots, after all India has over 2,700 of them. Last week, on Women's Day, a woman piloted one such flight sitting in the commander's seat—for the first time ever.

It was a helicopter flight from Juhu airport to Mumbai High. What was remarkable about that flight was that it made Pawan Hans' Captain Mayuri Deshmukh the first woman in India to fly in command on an offshore flight. "Offshore" merely means situated at sea at some distance from the shore; such as Mumbai High, India's largest oil field, located over 176km off the west coast of Mumbai.

In India, while hundreds of women pilots operate airline flights, over two dozen women pilots fly civilian helicopter flights and within that category, currently, only one woman pilot operates offshore flights.

"My father was an IAF helicopter pilot and my earliest memories of my fascination with helicopters come from watching him take off and land at runway strips," said Capt Deshmukh.

After earning a helicopter licence in 2008 from a Florida flying school, she worked with two private helicopter companies operating corporate flights before she joined Pawan Hans Ltd (PHL), the government PSU, in 2015.

For a year, she flew onshore across the vast and geographically diverse Indian terrain, from the hills of the North East to the islands of Andaman Nicobar, Naxalite holds in Gadchiroli; flying seven hours a day, gaining valuable experience transporting passengers from airports to inaccessible locations, providing last-mile connectivity.

Then in 2016, she completed offshore operations training. Being a male-dominated industry, she wasn't sure whether she would get to fly offshore. "But PHL gave me the opportunity," she said. "The first day I flew offshore to Mumbai High I was astounded to find the marvel that is the Mumbai High, miles and miles of metallic structures put up in the middle of the sea," she said. "You are landing on an elevated structure on the sea. It was one of the most beautiful experiences," she said.

Offshore flying can be rigorous, especially "production flying". "You fly 6-7 hours a day, transporting oil rig staff, doing 40-50 landings on oil rigs and platforms, with fuel and meal breaks in between," she said. Before each take-off comes the fuel and passenger load calculations and before each landing, there are wind speeds, visibility issues and obstructions to look out for. "Though twin engine helicopters are equipped with autopilot, we carry out manual landing," she said.

Oil rigs can appear like a men-only planet. "But ONGC ensured I get a separate, well-equipped room and toilet; they made proper arrangements for food and hygiene requirements," she said. "Offshore flying is a complex operation that demands skill and tenacity. If you can fly for hours in an aircraft that isn't air-conditioned, if you can let go of these small comforts, there is nothing that can stop you from joining this adventurous field," she said.

Mayuri Deshmukh earned a helicopter licence in 2008 from a Florida flying school

■ International Women's Day was celebrated at DFC's corporate office. RK Jain, MD, DFC addressed women employees. Renu P Chibber, GGM/Admin spoke on Gender Sensitisation & Workplace Harassment.

■ Capt Mayuri Deshmukh of Pawan Hans Ltd created history on Women's Day by becoming India's 1st Female Offshore Pilot in Command. Pawan Hans proudly congratulates her for making the nation proud.

Capt Mayuri is nation's first female offshore pilot

TIMES NEWS NETWORK

Mumbai: While airlines operated flights with all women crew to celebrate Women's Day, Pawan Hans Ltd (PHL), the public sector company that operates helicopters had its own quiet moment with history when its pilot Capt Mayuri Deshmukh became India's first female offshore Pilot-in-Command.

"Capt Deshmukh has been flying Dauphin AS 365 N3 helicopter for Pawan Hans for over seven years now. She is the first woman in India to fly in command off-shore," the helicopter operator said. "She is also the only woman in the country flying helicopters in offshore sector transporting the ONGC officials from Mumbai to the offshore platforms and oil rigs," Pawan Hans added. PHL has 120 pilots out of which four are women, said a PHL spokesperson. Unlike flying for an airline though, pilots employed with PHL operate flights for oil and gas exploration companies, police personnel, VIP flights, corporate flights

FLYING HIGH

and passenger transport in remote, border, hilly and inaccessible areas of North and North East India. "Capt Deshmukh is a highly experienced and qualified pilot and also has immense exposure of flying across different terrains of the country which includes Daman and Diu and Andaman and Nicobar Islands," said PHL.

ANDHRA PRADESH MEDICAL SERVICES & INFRASTRUCTURE DEVELOPMENT CORPORATION

Tender Notice No.21/APMSIDC/2021-22,   Dated:08.03.2022

APMSIDC invites tenders through e-procurement platform (https://tender.apeprocurement.gov.in) for Equipment Wing: 1. Procure and supply of 432 new vehicles for 104 MMU Services under Family Physician Concept 2. Procure and supply of Equipment and other items under ECRP II package 3. Procure and supply of Equipment and other items to various Govt. Hospitals in AP under different schemes of NHM Funds 4. Procure and supply of Medical Equipment to Teaching Hospitals under DME Plan Budget 5. Procure and supply of Lab equipment to establish a in-house facility 6. Procure and supply of Medical Equipment and other items under 15th Finance Grants 7. Establishment of Standardization of Labour Rooms at various facilities in Andhra Pradesh.

DIPR NO.729PP/KL/ADVT/1/1/2021-22 Dt.09.03.2022   Sd/- for Managing Director

Road safety drills for BEST drivers

Capt. Mayuri's attention was the flying in the offshore sector, which involves flying to fixed and moving decks and oil platforms in the seas. Despite the reservations about female pilots being able to cope with the demanding flying, she took the bold step of expressing an interest to fly for it and pursue it. With her company's efforts and ONGC's willingness, she got the opportunity to enter the field. The journey to become a Captain here was not an easy one, with intricate rules, a vast training syllabus, and physically demanding environments. It was a journey of years of hard work and determination to become a Captain against all the odds. She has now further embarked on the journey of joining the company's management as an Operations Manager (Coordination) for the Western Region.

Challenges

Entry into the field – Capt. Mayuri says, "A machine is handled based on skill so it doesn't matter whether it's a male or a female pilot. Back in 2009, the real struggle as a female pilot was to find a job. There were reservations in the mind of employers because the domain of helicopter flying is all about reaching where the mainstream modes of transport cannot reach. So most of the areas where helicopters fly are in small towns and remote places. To convince them that like any other field, there would be struggles, but one has to have an open mind to at least start somewhere was a little difficult. Of course, daily issues like sanitation and staying arrangements especially in the smaller places was all about keeping self-comfort on a back burner."

ON/OFF System – Unlike airlines, helicopter operations in the offshore industry follow an ON/OFF rostering pattern, with pilots working 6 weeks ON duty followed by 3 weeks OFF duty. The majority of helicopter operations take place between sunrise and sunset, with only a small percentage of operations taking place at night. One has to be prepared for long hours of work in the daytime. Flying is every day from morning to evening for 6 weeks. One has to make offshore a second home while on duty.

Psychological and Physiological Exhaustion – The degree of physical and mental weariness is quite a bit. Flying close to 7 hours with 30 to 40 landings per day can be quite exhausting. Landings and take-offs are manual, repetitive and fast-paced, whereas only cruising flights for a short duration are automated.

Job with family life – Since it's all about flying into lesser accessible areas, one has to be on the move and away from main cities. In return, one has to be able to create that extra space and time for family. So yes, it can be a little challenging but one can always work his/her way around it. A true aviator would know that the passion to fly is unrelenting.

Life at the oil platforms – The contracts require staying overnight at platforms and while efforts are made to increase comfort, it does become a little restrictive in nature. Except for emergencies, there is no mobile network or internet access. Because the accommodation floors are stacked on top of each other, one must constantly climb and descend multiple staircases. Also as a female, she has to stay in the accommodations overnight with all other men counterparts and share bathrooms/restrooms while on duty.

A journey upwards

Here's a story of a woman who had the opportunity to chase her dreams and at every point she faced a challenge, she turned it into a resolve to cross the path of 'Can I' to 'I can'. She won the following accolades in her journey:

1. Awarded by the Ministry of Civil Aviation in March 2022 for Excellence in the field of Offshore Flying.
2. Holds a Record in the Limca Book of Records (LBR) as the First Woman Offshore Captain.
3. Awarded by the Rotary Wing Society of India (RWSI) for Outstanding achievements in Civil Helicopter Industry.
4. Was actively involved in the Beti Padhao Beti Bachao programme in the Naxal areas of Gadchiroli to inspire tribal girls in these belts of Maharashtra while on duty.
5. Awarded by International Women Pilots' Association(IWPA), World Association of Women Warriors (WAOW) for excellence in Aviation.

Message to the readers

In today's times, it is not uncommon for women to be a part of aviation, a field which has warmly welcomed them for their truly deserving roles as well as their capabilities. It is a known fact that all the male pilots have been showing their exemplary skills and performing the arduous tasks of flying in offshore, but now a feather in the cap has been added to the domain of women aviators too when Capt. Mayuri Deshmukh is set to command and fly helicopters to this world of seas. Her unwavering dedication and exceptional skills have made this journey of hers an inspiring story for young women to pursue a career in helicopters as well.

She says, "The idea of clearance as a Pilot in Command should not be taken to highlight that it is a female pilot who did it and that's why it's creditworthy. The idea should be rather to

propagate that the field is as open to women as it is to men, if one is willing to put in the hard work. My seniors and colleagues are the ones who have groomed and nurtured me to arrive at this stage and I'm thankful for that".

Instagram handle: @cyclicpilot

Facebook: @mayuri.deshmukh.714

Email id: mayuridv@gmail.com

INDIA न्यूज़
National Woman
Pride Awards
2021
Mayhigh Films
Since 1985
CERTIFICATE
DR. KUILJEIT UPPAAL

Dr. Kuiljeit Uppaal

Worlds first image scientist impact strategist & CEO-KREA

"You can do anything you put your mind to – Be Unstoppable and Limitless!"

Dr. Kuiljeit Uppaal is the world's first image scientist and a renowned global personality who has brought immense honour to India in her area of work. Dr. Kuiljeit is a 'World Records India', 'Asia Book of Records', 'Bharat Book of World Records', and 'India Book of Records' holder for being the first image scientist in the world! She has won several international and national awards for innovation, education, and social impact, including the Karmaveer Chakra Award by the United Nations and iCongo; Bharat Keerti Award, 2022; Shiksha Bharti Award, 2020; World Innovation Award – Hall of Fame Honour, 2019; Maharashtra Ratna Puraskar 2023; Innovative Education Leadership Award – Excellence in Social Innovation & Global Impact 2019; WEF Exceptional Leader of Excellence Award 2021 amongst many others. She is a super-specialist in Persona & Image Management, Psychometrics, NLP, Personal Branding, Strategic Self-Management and Life Skills.

Dr. Kuiljeit has also been awarded the title of 'Genius Polymath', since she has expertise in multiple areas and has worn several hats, from being an image scientist, an impact strategist, a creative director, a pilot, and an entrepreneur to an author and an educationist amongst others.

Her journey has been truly inspirational, and she has lived life as stark evidence of her core thought that she shares with the world "You can do anything you put your mind to – Be Unstoppable and Limitless!"

Dr. Kuiljeit's challenges started as a young infant who was afflicted with polio in her leg and was made to realise it by her peers as she grew that she was different and not good enough. She was often made fun of, while she helplessly limped. And then, her turning point happened one day as a little girl, when she shared her agony and confusion with her father about why people ridiculed her and what was wrong with her! Her father emphatically told her that 'nothing was wrong with her' and she could do anything she puts her mind to! That

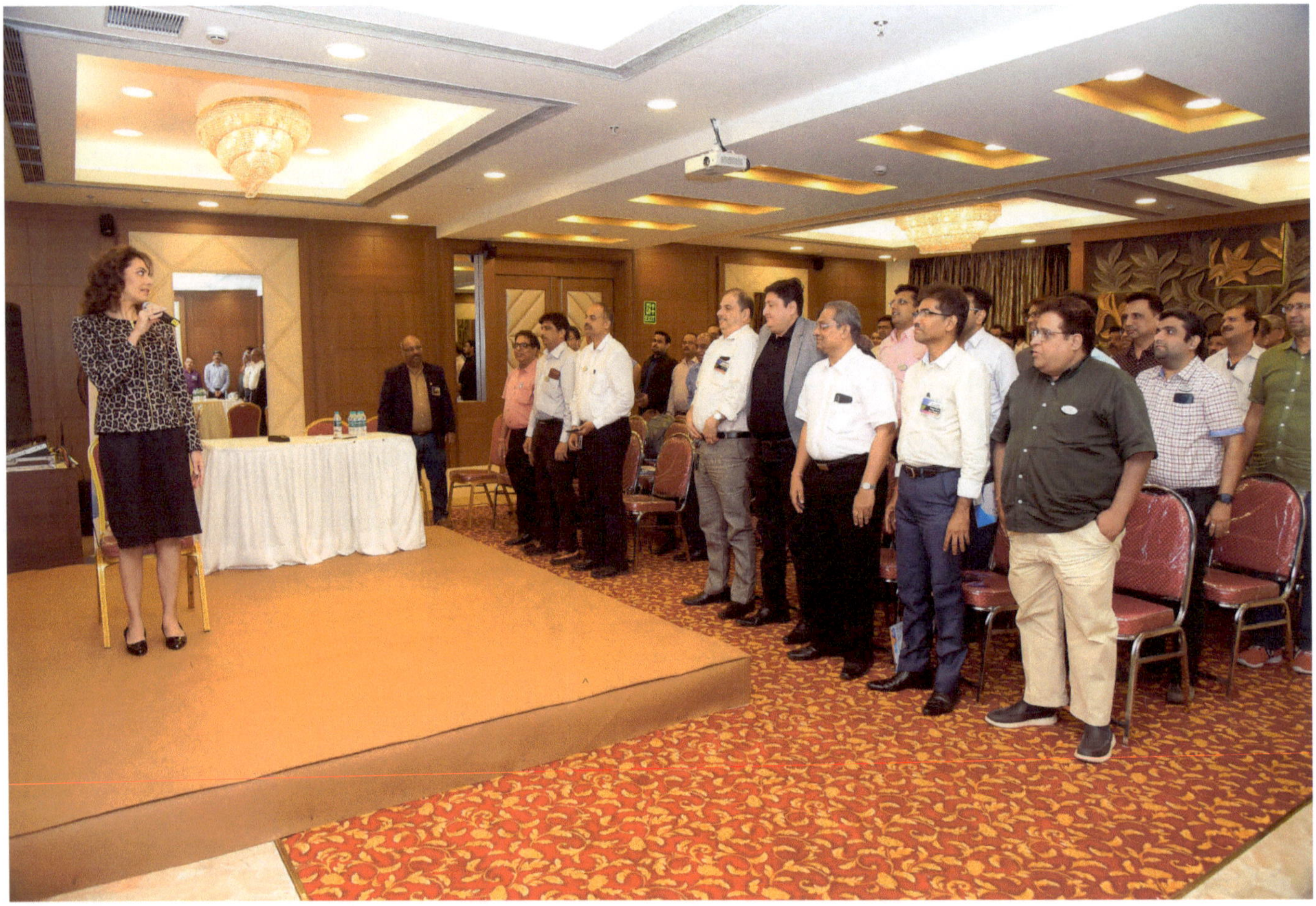

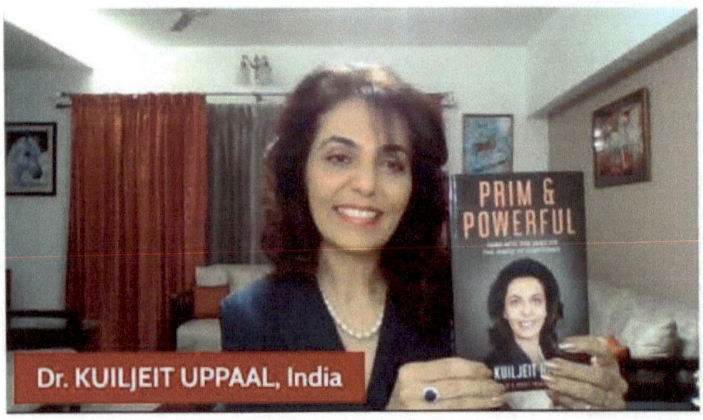

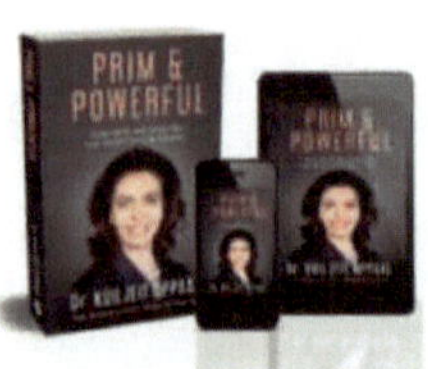

LIVE 36:03
BOOK LAUNCH
PRIM & POWERFUL
Dr. KUILJEIT UPPAAL
THE WORLD'S FIRST IMAGE SCIENTIST & IMPACT STRATEGIST
Dr. KUILJEIT UPPAAL, India
Rajkumar Hirani
/Dr.Kuiljeit Uppaal
Order your book now on
amazon
Unveiling 'PRIM & POWERFUL'... Momentous moment !

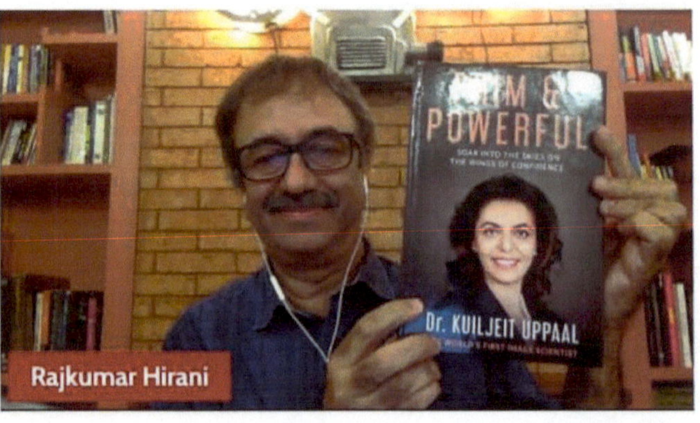

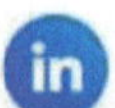

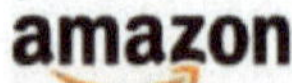

sentence became her gospel truth for life and soon she became a positive and powerful disruptor in life. She worked very hard on strengthening the affected leg, and over the next few years became an Indian classical dancer, a gymnast, a sports champion for multiple sports and a national-level athlete, a parade commander in the paramilitary forces, and even a pilot. There was no looking back for this amazing and determined fighter! The same people who had ridiculed her now followed her footsteps admiringly, as their role model.

Curiosity and learning have always been integral to her personality, because of which the zeal to learn new concepts and master new domains has been a constant all through her life. While at school, she excelled in almost every sort of intellectual, cultural, or sports competition; she had also indirectly mastered the art of delving into multiple things alongside academics. Her interests diversified to music, creative writing, painting, poetry, adventure sports, lending her voice, and a plethora of things, and the only constant that clung to her was the beauty of 'change'.

Dr. Kuiljeit is driven by excellence, integrity and giving a 100% to everything she does, despite the odds. She believes that she is her own benchmark, and her goal is always to beat her last performance and be her best version every single day.

In about three decades of work experience across diverse industries like aviation education, advertising, media, IT, research, and academia, she demonstrated the unique and rare ability to traverse comfortably from one industry to another, and with utmost humility, because every time it meant 'leaving one industry at a highpoint in rank, and starting off in another from almost the bottom of the pyramid like a fresher'. Being married to an Army Officer, she knew she had limitations of longevity in any organisation, because every few years, her husband would get transferred to a new place, and her professional journey would come to a halt, until she would reignite it in a brand-new place and a new industry. In the zest and zeal to make the most of every tenure, she worked ten times harder and faster than her peers and rose to higher management positions within extraordinarily short durations. This was no mean feat!

She has been an amazing outlier with a diverse journey; she operates with her combination of 3 Zs: Zero ego, Zeal to learn, and Zest for life and evolution. This is demonstrated by her widened horizon of perspectives in every way and her vast and diverse knowledge base. She is also a very balanced and rounded individual, personally and professionally.

In her corporate tenure, her immense potential, hard work, and growth often made her a victim of envy and jealousy of her peers and seniors. But undaunted, she stayed focussed on being relevant by constantly investing in herself, especially with regard to knowledge and know-how, which she felt is the best technical differentiator; she ensured that she always had a 'One-Up' in this sphere. She mastered the art of multitasking and interpersonal skills and was one of the most respected and loved names in all the organisations she was part of. By now she has built for herself a person's most tangible and marketable asset – a great reputation!

After nearly three decades of work and at the apex of her corporate career, Dr. Kuiljeit happily turned to 'entrepreneurship with a purpose' because she had a calling to make a positive difference in the image of the youth, women, and professionals of India. Over the decades of her work experience, she had noticed a 'commonality' in professionals across industries and at various levels, the lack of 'making an impact', be it their communication, presentation, behaviour, mindset, self-worth, belief, and other such variables. This visible deficiency urged her to find credible solutions to help the population of her country. In order to ensure that she disseminates legit and valid knowledge to the world, she delved into the depth of research with a PhD in a pristine area of academia and pioneered the Science of PRIM (Persona & Image Management) through scientific study and empirical testing over years of research. She has created several new scientific concepts and innovations, including D-PRIM, PRIMEA, PIT Model, and TILSOM Framework amongst others, as well as the world's first PIQ (Persona & Image Quotient), and continually generates new ammunition for entrepreneurship and social impact in global society.

Dr. Kuiljeit started her PSR and dynamic mission, 'PRIM Worldwide: Mission Possible' to make a positive difference to the persona and image of the youth and women of India and across the globe. She has trained tens of thousands of youth and faculty from the higher education segment as part of her ongoing mission. She intends to continue to reach out to every possible individual, especially girls and boys who are relatively economically challenged, in this journey of hers and make a positive difference in their lives.

Alongside, she decided to enhance human capital in organisations through personality development, soft skills, and behavioural training for higher productivity and effectiveness through her training venture Krea, for which she has an august list of clientele.

Being the pioneer of the Science of PRIM, she understands that the world now looks towards her for a constant feed of knowledge and academic sharing of her subject. She has written research papers in Emerald and Scopus-indexed reputed international journals as well as book chapters for renowned publication houses like Springer. Apart from having contributed to a few

DR. KUILJEIT UPPAAL WITH THE FIRST LADY OF CYPRUS MRS ANDRI ANASTASIADES

hundred educational books on entrepreneurship, personality development, aviation, customer service, communication etc., Dr. Kuiljeit has also authored 'PRIM & POWERFUL', the world's first-ever book in PRIM, which guides and facilitates individuals to become a more confident, self-reliant, powerful, and incredible version of themselves, using concepts devised from her extensive research in the area, over the years.

Being a first-generation entrepreneur, Dr. Kuiljeit discovered a new journey of watching the world through a different lens. While people constantly reminded her that entrepreneurship is not worth it and she should get back to a regular job, she moved ahead with the inner strength of 'never giving up', even though there was no one to guide or support her venture. She faced several setbacks, including financial constraints and serious health challenges. But as much as she stumbled 'n' number of times, she bounced back and held on relentlessly like a Braveheart! She asserts with a calm smile,

"Challenges don't come to destroy you, they come as opportunities to discover your hidden potential and strengths, so embrace them as friends."

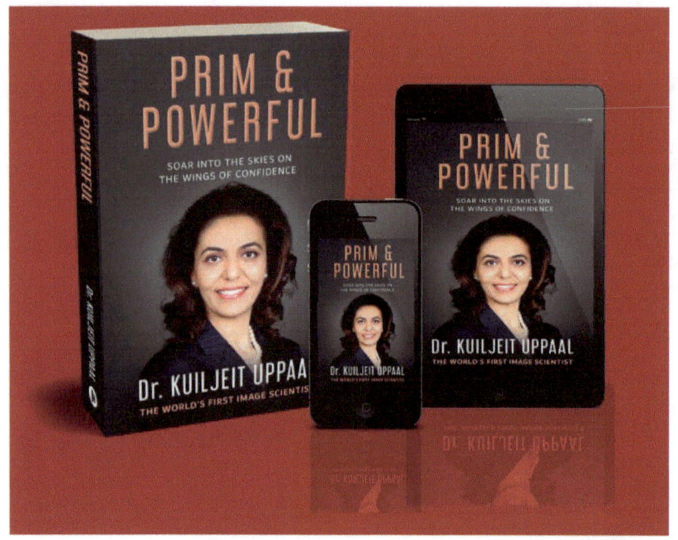

Today, she is applauded as a distinguished 'Scientistpreneur', an internationally acclaimed impact strategist and one of the top ten emerging entrepreneurs in India. Apart from a long list of corporate clientele, she also mentors celebrities, public figures, C-suite and management professionals, business owners, and professionals from all walks of life across the world.

Dr. Kuiljeit extended her entrepreneurship experiences by being an independent director certified by IICA, Ministry of Corporate Affairs, Government of India. She is also an advisor/office bearer of many women's organisations around the world and works towards bringing about policies and creating a robust ecosystem for the empowerment of the youth and women globally.

This amazing impact strategist has made India proud in her area, apart from being a thought leader and inspirational humanitarian who has been impacting thousands of lives globally on her mission to make a powerful difference to the persona and image of individuals and enhance life skills across the globe. Dr. Kuiljeit is passionate about contributing to global society through the UNSDGs and has been contributing towards UNSDG 4: Quality Education, for which she has received the Global Goals Award 2021. She has often shared her thoughts and ideas on several international forums that work towards the United Nations' goals.

Dr. Kuiljeit's commendable journey from a young child afflicted with polio and unsure about her abilities to breaking all barriers and becoming a 'Genius Polymath' and the world's first image scientist stands testimony to the words 'Unstoppable and Limitless'.

She is a true daughter of the soil and an incredible inspiration for all.

www.linkedin.com/in/dr-kuiljeituppaal

insta/Dr.kuiljeit.uppaal

Email-info@kuiljeituppaal.com

www.kuiljeituppaal.com

CONSULATE SYED ALGAZI

Consulate Syed Algazi

His Excellency Nawab Syed Algazi, Honorary Consul of the Republic of Liberland (Europe), Chairman and Managing Director, N.F. Constructions India-Dubai, Founder & Chairperson, Braveheart MARTYRS Foundation

Any Dream Can Become Reality Through Hard Work, Dedication and Firm Determination

His Excellency Nawab Syed Algazi belongs to the royal and great noble family of Hyderabad. He is the great-grandson of Nawab Fakhr ul Mulk Bahadur who built great palaces (Errum Manzil Palace), monuments (Tomb of Nawab Fakhr ul Mulk–known as the Taj Mahal of Hyderabad Deccan), Nizam Collage and many other palaces around Hyderabad Deccan. He is also the great-grandson of Salar Jung III (maternal) and nephew of Prince Mouzzam Jah, 2nd son of 7th Nizam.

His Excellency Nawab Syed Algazi continues the family business and tradition since the past 37 years. He started his entrepreneur's journey at the very young age of 16 in 1986 with **$67.40 (Rs. 5000 INR)** in his pocket. He provided employment to a number of boys at that time who were unable to make ends meet. He is an alumnus of one of the top 5 military schools of India, Rashtriya Military School Bangalore, 1979 batch, which consist of his school batch mates Lt. General CP Cariappa (Ex-Military secretary to the President of India, great Armed forces hero Col. DPK Pillay, bureaucrats like Baba Kalyani, Chairman of Bharat Forge and above all,his school seniors like S. Jaishankar Minister of External Affairs of India, Ajit Kumar Doval National Security Advisor of India.

His Excellency Nawab Syed Algazi is the chairman and founder of 'N.F. Constructions Pvt. Ltd.', which is into the construction field since

1991 and has its corporate offices in Hyderabad, India, and Dubai; he has a business presence in 14 Countries and a vast experience of 37 years. He is in the process of collaborating internationally in UAE, Europe, Africa, and India for a few projects in pharmaceutical, construction, tea, and other sectors, and has partnered with top UAE developers.

He is also the founder of the Braveheart Martyrs Foundation.

He was officially appointed as India's youngest Honorary Consul General of the Republic of Liberland in India. His tenure began in May 2023.

Life of a Dreamer

Today he may be seen swinging and driving to his offices in India and Dubai in swanky BMWs, Ferraris, or Lamborghinis, but he started his journey with just **$67.40 (Rs.5000 INR)** in his pocket and it took him 37 years of dedication and hard work to reach where he is today. So, we take an in-depth look into his life which can be an example for the younger generation who dream.

As a child, His Excellency Syed Algazi was extraordinary and wise. He excelled in everything he did. He was a perfectionist. Whether it was studies, sports, or dramatics, he was the best. He was a restless soul ready to prove to the world a point that he has arrived. He is a bundle of strength, intelligence, and high ideologies. He is a dreamer, but with a difference. Whatever he dreams, he sees to it that his dreams become a reality through hard work, dedication, and firm determination till his dreams become reality.

Although he belongs to the royal family of Hyderabad and had a lavish life to enjoy his

youthful days, he preferred to be a self-made person, and at the very young age of 16 years, in 1986, he took $67.40 (Rs.5000INR) from his mother and started a business on his own. In a year's time, he launched Hyderabad and Andhra Pradesh's first air-conditioned video games arcade. It was inaugurated by the then Indian cricket team captain, Mohd. Azharuddin. The videogames were brought from Hong Kong and he provided employment to a number of boys at that time who were unable to meet the ends. With the launch of video games, mushrooming started and in a few years, hundreds of centres were started who copied him and started making video games in Hyderabad. By that time, His Excellency Syed Algazi got disinterested; however, he still had 6 to 7 video game arcades already running in Hyderabad.

He was surrounded by politicians, film stars, cricketers, and people from all walks of life due to his mother being a journalist from the 1970s. As a journalist and critic, she used to meet many a stars like Dilip Kumar, Nargis Dutt, Sunil Dutt, Dharmendra, Amitabh Bachchan, Hema Malini, Jeetender, Vinod Khanna, Sanjay Dutt, Anil Kapoor and many more and hence, they were very friendly. His Excellency Syed Algazi's childhood was spent among glamorous Bollywood personalities, powerful politicians, and top cricketers.

His Excellency Syed Algazi had a fascination for cricket and boxing. As years passed, he flourished in cricket up to the state level, and every weekend his photo appeared in leading newspapers. He is still known for his batting skill and 24 hundreds. In 1991, he was playing for Hyderabad in senior Zonals, and VVS Laxman happened to get out on 99 and was crying. His Excellency Syed Algazi pacified him as his Captain and teammate. As a matter of fact, His Excellency Syed Algazi was selected as the cricket captain of the country club when they launched their cricket team. On the inauguration of the cricket academy, he was lucky to share the same platform with greats like Sunil Gavaskar and Kapil Dev. After the inauguration, he and Mr. Sunil Gavaskar had a chat for a long time in his hotel room in Taj Banjara, which resulted in His Excellency Syed Algazi hitting that era's highest individual score of 186.

By this time His Excellency Syed Algazi got interested in interior designing and furniture business and opened a showroom with big fanfare, which was inaugurated by the then sports minister Mrs. Geeta Reddy and was attended by VVIPS, film stars, and cricketers. The furniture business still continues. In the meantime, his mother asked him to construct a farmhouse which had become an in-thing in Hyderabad. His Excellency Syed Algazi planned the design of the building, landscaping, garden, pantry and other details, got the plan sanctioned and implemented the same. He made it with such passion, vision, and hard work that when everyone finally saw the farmhouse, they said in one breath that it is one of the best farmhouses in Hyderabad. Right from the beautiful entrance, kitchen, garden, big lawns, huge swimming pool, plantation to the modern building, everything was very beautiful. Then he realised how much potential he had in him to become a builder.

The next venture on his hand was a palatial well-designed beautifully elevated bungalow at Banjara Hills. He got the three-storied building completed in 10 months' time and the final product was beyond dreams and expectations. Even big wigs praised his efforts. His parents' friend, a senior Congress minister said when he visited his place, "I feel like I am sitting in Akbar's Darbar". His Excellency Syed Algazi proved the saying "Jack of all master of none" wrong. Whatever he did in his life has become a masterpiece.

Once His Excellency Nawab Syed Algazi casually met a boy called Saleem who was working as an area manager with Deli 9 at Ibn Battuta Mall in Dubai. From him, His Excellency Syed Algazi got the inspiration to open a coffee shop "Mr. Donald" at Begumpet, Hyderabad. He spent 3 months in planning the exclusive interiors, first-class furniture, imported machines, and the best staff. By the end of 3 months, he got the coffee shop inaugurated by Indian cricket captain Mohd. Azharuddin, who happens to be a family friend in style and again everyone was astonished to see a foreign-style place ready. It was a beautiful experience watching him glow while giving interviews to television and media people. He did it again single-handedly.

He has adopted an orphanage and has been helping the orphans and underprivileged kids in a very positive and realistic way, for which he has established a charitable trust "Sadiqa Sultana Charitable Trust" and has been doing his bit for many social causes for 37 years, which has never been spoken about or shown to the outer world. He is such a down-to-earth and shy person that he is petrified to pieces to talk about himself, his work, and his company in media and believes in keeping a low profile. He donates 20% of his earnings that comes from his construction business.

1999: The war and sacrifices that changed His Excellency Syed Algazi's life into an Indian patriot

It was the month of June 1999 when the Kargil War broke out due to the infiltration of our neighbouring country's army, which resulted in India losing 527 soldiers. The bloodshed of our Jawans left a very deep impact on his mind and heart and, this was the time when His Excellency Syed Algazi took an oath to do something for our martyr war heroes and their families. The restlessness of forming a foundation took birth. It took nearly 17 years for him to go deep into finding the details of thousands of martyrs' and war heroes' families, not just Kargil War heroes. As there was no social media during those years, finding so many war heroes' families was an uphill task. Ultimately, after a lot of hard work and dedication put in for years, he started contacting many veer naris (War Widows) across India. He single-handedly found what he was looking for for ages.

Although he was doing his bit all these years for war heroes, society and humanity with his charitable trust named after his respected mother, Barrister Mrs. Sadiqa Sultana, Sadiqa Sultana Charitable Trust, he was restless to do something really big and good for our war heroes' families. It was during this time that he met all the great Generals, Lt. Generals, Majors, Colonels of our nation in different seminars and conclaves in Delhi as he himself is a Cadet of the Rashtriya Military School Bangalore and Lt. General CP Cariappa (Ex-Military Secretary to the president of India Shri. Ram Nath Kovind) and Col. DPK Pillay are his batch mates.

After meeting them and knowing all the small details and issues about what a private entity can do for our Indian Armed Forces to make a difference in their lives, His Excellency Syed Algazi thought of a foundation which would officially do some progressive and patriotic work towards our country and war heroes' families. He founded Braveheart Martyrs Foundation (BMF) and his patriotic journey began. Today, The Braveheart Martyrs Foundation endeavours to be a platform and a bridge between the citizens and the martyrs' families.

Accomplishments of His Excellency Syed Algazi:

1. He was named the youngest entrepreneur of Hyderabad in Andhra Pradesh in 1987 (present-day Telangana) by the Indian Chamber of Commerce Delhi at the early age of 19.
2. His Excellency Syed Algazi has been invited twice to the president's estate, Rashtrapati Bhavan, Delhi, for his wonderful, selfless, and dedicated services towards the Indian Armed Forces & Martyrs' families all across India.

3. He is credited for initialising the initiative for the first-ever war memorial in Telangana history by a civilian cadet since the formation of the TRS Government, Telangana Rashtra Samithi in 2014.

4. He is also the first civilian in the history of Telangana and Andhra Pradesh to be awarded by high-ranking Army officials at HQ 35 Infantry Brigade Vasant Vihar, New Delhi, for his services towards Indian Armed Forces, martyrs and their families all across India.

5. He is also the recipient of the Rajiv Gandhi Award for his services towards the Indian Armed Forces, martyrs and their families and his initiatives and campaigns across the globe.

6. On 4 September 2019, His Excellency Syed Algazi became the first personality in the history of Telangana and Andhra Pradesh to be awarded the Sir Syed Ahmad Award by the Aligarh University for his contribution to the nation, martyrs' families and social work all across India.

7. He is also credited for the initiative of forming the Telangana Police Youth Club on 18 March 2018.

8. His Excellency Syed Algazi has initiated many campaigns and honouring programmes all across the globe called Golden Salute Honouring our Martyr Heroes, their families, veer naris, war and living legends. The first Golden Salute honouring programme was held at Hyderabad on 2 December 2018, which was followed by Delhi, New York, New Jersey, Chandigarh, Bangalore, Belgaum, Ajmer, Chail, Dholpur, Pune, Jammu and other cities in 2019.

9. His Excellency Syed Algazi was honoured and recognised by the Embassy of the Islamic Republic of Afghanistan at a glittering programme at Trident for the good work he has been doing through his company, N.F. Constructions and NGO Braveheart Martyrs Foundation for three decades.

10. His Excellency Syed Algazi has been awarded with the International Entrepreneur of the Year on 25 August 2021 by the Global Business Icons for his wonderful international business and social achievements of 37 years.

11. His Excellency Syed Algazi was honoured by the royal family office of UAE in Dubai.

Mission and Vision:

To change the lives of 20,000 families of the Indian Armed Forces, the police force, and civilians and to look after their kids' education and scholarship with the help from national and international organisations and government bodies.

1. As His Excellency Syed Algazi is a cadet from Rashtriya Military School Bangalore (one of the five top military schools followed by Ajmer, Chail, Dholpur, and Belgaum and all are called and known as Georgians), he thus has the support of approximately 50,000 Georgian families from all around the globe who will be coming forward to help him do something very substantial, progressive work for around 20,000 armed forces personnel, martyrs, and their families.

2. His Excellency Syed Algazi had also organised a flood relief cricket match at Lal Bahadur Stadium in 1991 as he himself was a professional cricket player and played for 29 years for Hyderabad. Thus, it was easy for him to call his friends Sachin Tendulkar and Sunil Gavaskar. This was the only match where both these legends played together, and Kapil Dev, Mohammed Azharuddin, Arshad Ayyub and many other Indian cricketers of that era also participated. Mr. Syed Algazi was also the captain of the cricket team of which Indian player VVS Laxman was a part in 1991. He was also the captain of the Country Club Hyderabad when they launched their cricket team. On the inauguration of the cricket academy, he shared the same platform with cricket legends like Sunil Gavaskar, Kapil Dev, and Sachin Tendulkar.

3. His Excellency Syed Algazi has been an active member and has organised many social events like a cricket match at Lal Bahadur Stadium in Hyderabad between Bollywood and Tollywood film personalities in 1989 in aid of the flood-affected victims. Here, he happened to meet and interact with all the big film personalities like the late Sunil Dutt, Dharmendra, the late Vinod Khanna, Sanjay Dutt, Danny, late Amjad Khan, Madhuri Dixit, Juhi Chawla, the late Sridevi, Jaya Prada, Chiranjeevi, Krishna, Venkatesh, Nagarjuna, Arjun, Rajender Prasad, Meena, Roja, and many other superstars.

4. His Excellency Syed Algazi has taken up many causes like women empowerment and child development.

GOLDEN SALUTE: HONOURING OUR WAR HEROES ACROSS THE GLOBE

1. For the first time in the history of Telangana and Andhra Pradesh, on 2 December 2018 at Radisson Hotel Hitech City, Hyderabad, 25 of our martyrs, veer naris, living war legends including the likes of Captain Vikram Batra (Param Vir Chakra Kargil War), Major Padmapani Acharya (Maha Vir Chakra Kargil War), Vijayant Thapar (Vir Chakra), Captain Anuj Nayar (Maha Vir Chakra Kargil War), Captain Haneef Uddin (Vir Chakra Kargil War), Captain Sumeet Roy (Vir Chakra Kargil War), Respected Lt. General Hari Prasad to name a few were honoured.

2. His Excellency Syed Algazi honoured 40 veer naris and families of martyrs, war legends, and living heroes from all across the country with Golden Salute 2 in Delhi on 6 July 2019.

3. His Excellency Syed Algazi and Braveheart Martyrs Foundation in association with the Federation of Indian Associations New York, New Jersey, Connecticut, and the Consulate General India, New York, honoured 10 Indian martyr war heroes and living legends in New York City in a first of its kind honouring programme in the history of USA called 'Golden Salute 3'.

Taare Zameen Par – Dil Se: India's biggest virtual live programme with great martyr war heroes' families and living legends was held on 13 June 2020. War heroes came under one umbrella from all across the globe (New York, New Jersey,

Chandigarh, Palampur, Dwarka, Delhi, Noida, KSA, London Dubai, Bangalore, Germany, Lucknow) in a never seen before extravaganza.

BMF WAR MEMORIAL: CLICK HERE TO PAY YOUR TRIBUTES: www. braveheartmartyrs.com

India's first pre- and post-independence era's online war memorial with a difference. A dream initiative and mission of His Excellency Syed Algazi. BMF was launched by the great families of our war heroes where one can submit their tributes to our great Martyr War Heroes from 1948 to 2020.

No Indian civilian has done so much of patriotic programmes and work for our martyr war heroes' families, living legends, and veer naris (war widows) than His Excellency Syed Algazi. He is loved and blessed by the families of innumerable Param Vir Chakra, Maha Vir Chakra, Vir Chakra, Shaurya Chakra awardees and living legends for his extraordinary and selfless services towards our motherland and the Indian Armed Forces.

There is a saying for him in Telangana, "If there is anyone in India who wants to know something in Telangana State about our soldiers, veterans and martyrs then the road leads to His Excellency Syed Algazi and Braveheart Martyrs Foundation's door." For his impact and kindness, he has been given the title of "Patriot" by respected Ms. Swapna Roy, the great sacrificing mother of Kargil war hero, Captain Sumeet Roy (Vir Chakra).

28 April 2020: During the tough times of COVID-19, His Excellency Syed Algazi has quietly helped the needy and poor with $35508.92 (Rs.26, 44,000 (twenty-six lakhs and forty-four thousand rupees only)) worth of essentials to around 2600 people in India as his humanitarian efforts.

7 July 2020: His Excellency Syed Algazi offered his plot of approximately 3 acres on Gandipet Main Road in Hyderabad, Telangana, worth Rs. 5 to 7 crores for the purpose of COVID-19 patients' temporary quarantine.

Projects completed:

1. Azam's Castle
2. More than 50 projects in Dubai as a business partner for top developers of UAE.
3. Green Crystal Farms
4. Neha Villa
5. Azam's Castle 2
6. Golf Edge 26th floor
7. Appajiguda Farm
8. Kismatpur Garden
9. Lake View Cinema
10. Suncity Villas and Bungalows

Upcoming Project: 48 projects from different developers of UAE and Azam's Castle 3 at Golden Heights Colony in Hyderabad, India.

The family legacy still continues after 224 years

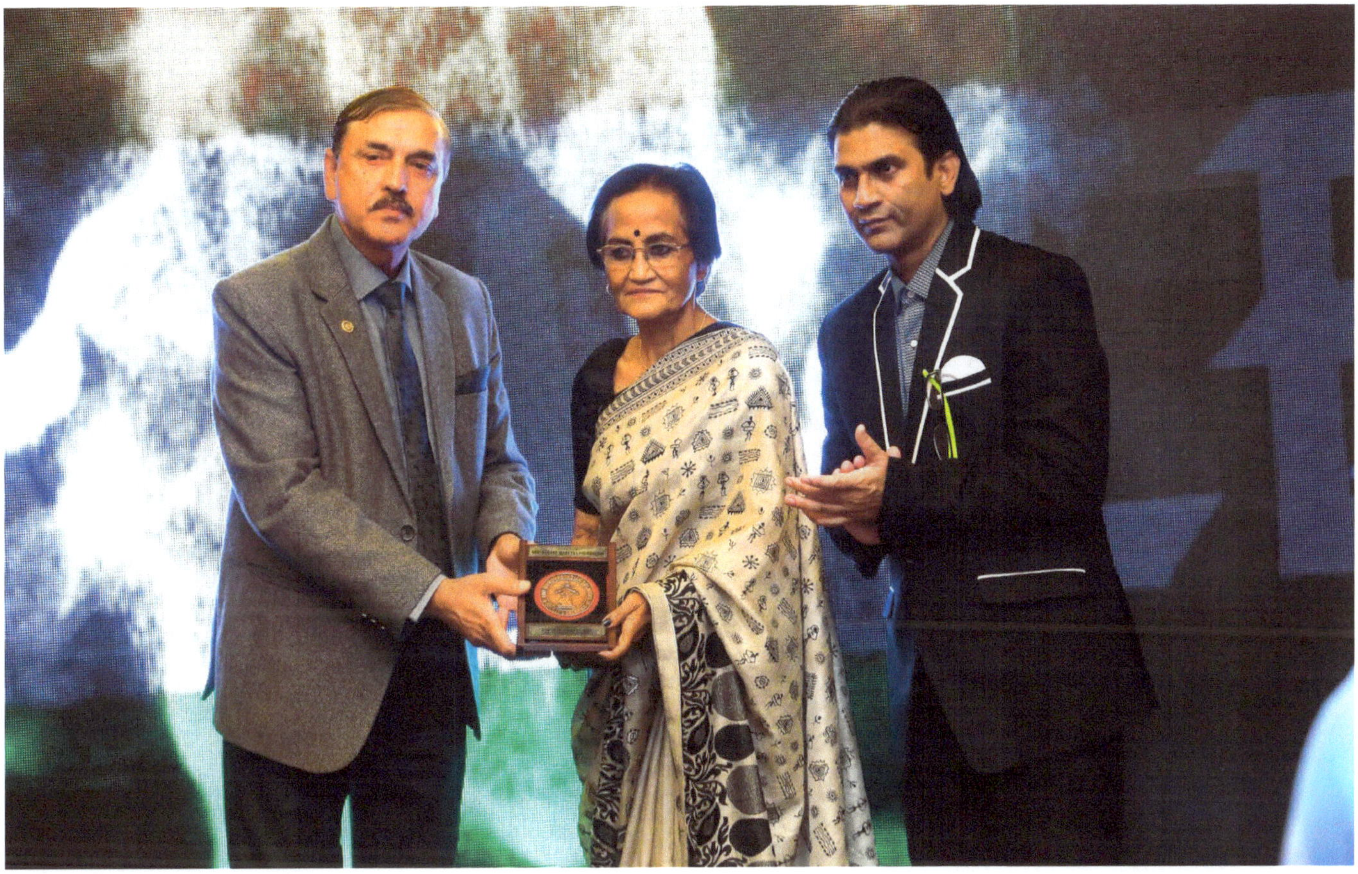

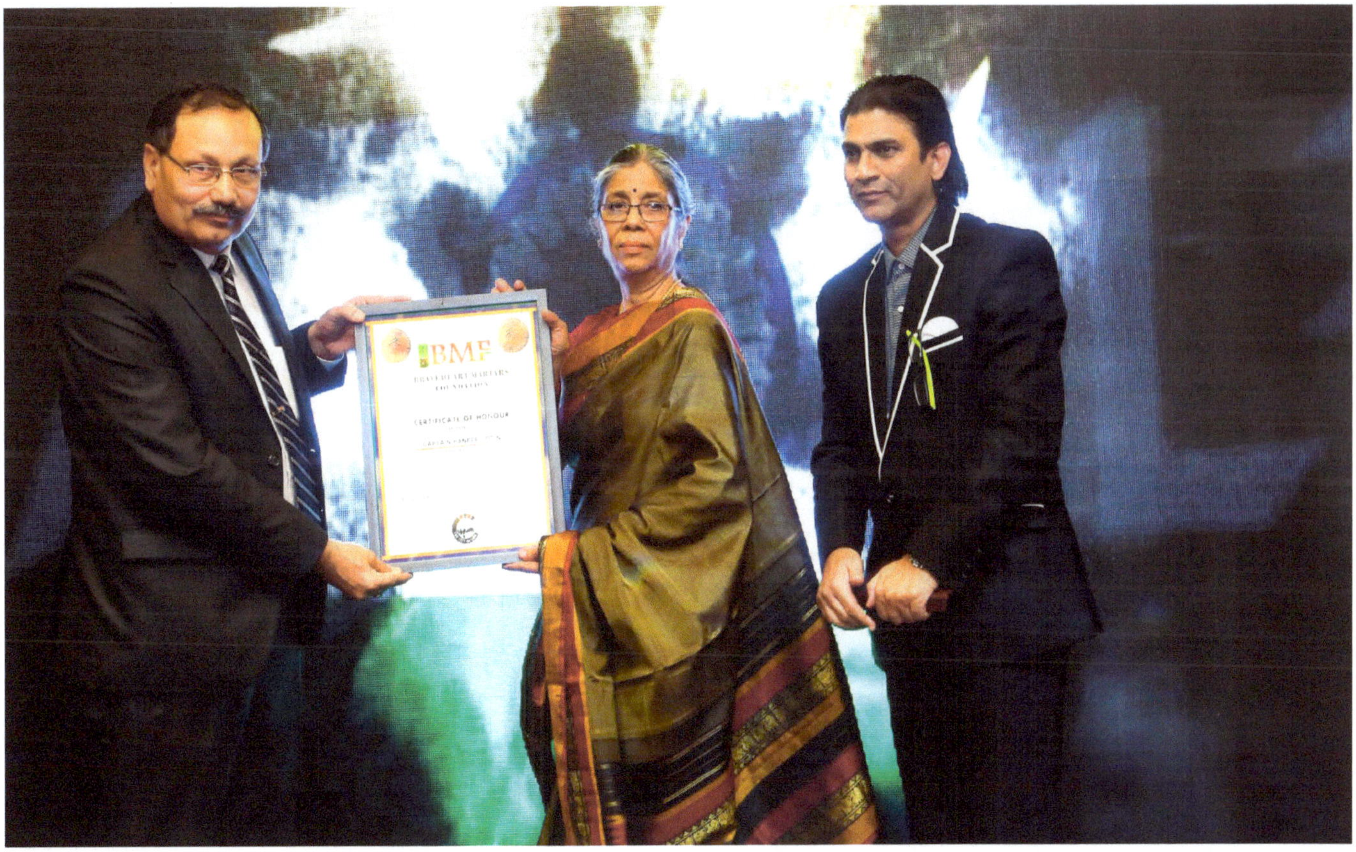
BMF
CERTIFICATE OF HONOUR

NEELAM BERRY

Neelam Berry

Managing Director Cistula Tulip Films Writer and Producer of Films

> # "Optimism is a happiness magnet. If you stay positive, good things and good people will be drawn to you."
>
> —*Mary Lou Retton*

Neelam Berry is a woman of substance. Her life is inspiring and interesting. She is always passionate about whatever she does. She calls her life luck by chance. As a child, she was very creative. She started writing stories and shayaris in Urdu. Her father always encouraged her to write. Her father is a learned individual and she learned a lot from him.

At an early age, she was an expert in dancing and playing Sitar. She took part in professional dramas and played Sitar in different functions. During college days, she found the man of her dreams, to whom she got married. After marrying the person of her choice, her journey started in a very different manner. She became a mother to her first son Karan; the motherhood experience was very beautiful and enjoyable. She believes that motherhood makes every woman wise and mature. By the time she joined her husband's well-renowned production company, she started learning everything about filming and production. Her husband Mr. Mike Berry always encouraged her to write.

Life is full of ups and downs. Sometimes circumstances outside your control appear and try to knock you off your feet, and it can be hard to find a silver lining in anything. Looking out at the world around us, it can be easy to get cynical that anything will change or that we have the power to make an impact. It's hard to fight the glass-half-empty mentality when life seems darker, but we learn from the past and plan for the future while staying in present.

She got an opportunity to write a story from a very prominent writer Amrita Pritam ji. She was asked to write the screenplay for the Doordarshan film titled 'Humsafar'. As the story was based on an old era, Neelam wrote the entire story with the consent of Amrita Pritam ji, the screenplay and the telefilm came out very well and was appreciated by the industry and audience. The telefilm was written and also produced by Neelam. With this, Neelam launched her company Golden Tulip Films. After this, she wrote numerous stories and screenplays for national and international media houses. Her company started producing serials, documentaries, telefilms, etc. for regional and foreign channels.

Neelam always wrote about life journey, realistic and related to the journey of a common woman. In her stories, there were no villains, no negative characters. Only TIME used to be the main character. Due to this, her stories were valued and cherished. Neelam always believes that everything happens for a reason and you just have to have faith in God's process. She believes in the saying, 'Man Proposes and God Disposes', which

means people can make plans; God determines how things will turn out.

Neelam was blessed with her second son, Shivaz in the year 1997, a huge gap of more than 10 years between both sons. Both Mike and Neelam were busy in their professional careers. The company was busy making and producing series and documentaries. One day, the company's senior production manager fell sick at the beginning of a huge project; so, Neelam Berry took the ropes in her hand and got into the new role of chief of productions. During this, she was able to understand the know-how of the production and its verticals. Daily gratitude can bring awareness of the small and also profound things in your life that are daily gifts.

The journey of her life was moving fast, and she was enjoying every aspect. She always

SHEconnects
WOMEN OF SUBSTANCE
HEconnects
Talented Menpreneurs Network
BUSINESS
CONFERENCE
CERTIFICATE

believes in the process of work rather than focusing on the results. She experienced many ups and downs, but she always used to go as per the flow of nature. She kept writing and making films, documentaries, advertisements, short films, etc. Neelam is very passionate about what she does, regardless of whatever comes in her journey.

She loves the journey of her life; she accepts challenges and ensures she completes it with full passion. She has been successful in both her professional and personal life.

At this stage, she is following her two other passions, fashion and cooking. Apart from her production company, she is a jury member in many fashion shows and beauty pageants. In many shows, she is a national mentor too, which reflects

an amazing achievement. She is also working with a couple of NGOs; one of the NGOs recently organised a beauty pageant for woman cancer survivors. She was an important part of the event and is very proud to be associated with such an event.

As a human being, Neelam has grown to be a passionate writer, poet, line producer, jury to Emmy Awards, USA, jury member in many beauty pageants and social worker. She believes that she is blessed with many things in her beautiful life. At this stage and age, she is very energetic, and she states that she is still in the learning phase.

Now, Neelam is living her life successfully professionally and following her dreams passionately. She is filled with enthusiasm and motivational thoughts. Her high level of motivation comes from her family who always motivated and encouraged her to follow her dreams and passions.

She dedicates her success to her father Prem Sharma, her husband Mike Berry, her sons, Karan and Shivaz, her daughter-in-law Sunaina and her granddaughter Liana.

Neelam's motto of life is 'Be Positive'. Your mind is more powerful than you think. What is down in the well comes up in the bucket. Fill yourself with positive things.

HEMA PAUL

Hema Paul

Founder & MD FEMVINGS

> **Saving a human from diseases and ill health is not the job of only a doctor, a nurse, or a caretaker. Taking care starts at home, with and by family members**
>
> *Hema Paul*

The *fitoor* to work for women's health is my driving force.

What can be said about Hema's journey of being padwoman; it has only been an undeterred march towards her goal. Belonging to a middle-class Indian family and married in a middle-class family, her second innings as a homemaker was all about difficult times and numerous hurdles.

Taking you back to the days when she was quite popular as a marketing professional at Oswal Group. Upon completion of her professional courses in Computer Application and Management, Hema started her journey as a marketing professional. With discipline, dedication, and sheer devotion as her strength and forte, she excelled over time and was soon awarded a promotion for leading a huge marketing network for the organisation.

Now, you may think that her devotion and passion to be a notable professional might be the reason for her to start her venture FemVings, but it was her love and willingness to serve the vulnerable section of Indian women. And as we say, a hurdle race is not a hurdle race till you get to pass more than one challenge, her journey was definitely one of those races; the most difficult one to pass was to get her project approved by the Government of India. Crossing all the challenges successfully, she has now established a sanitary manufacturing unit FemVings under the Ministry of Micro, Small, and Medium Enterprises, Government of India under the guidance of implementing agency, KVIC, Govt. of India.

Hema often narrates her story of ups and downs post marriage, which led her to take the path of being a homemaker, and how in spite of all that, she is undeterred in her focus and passion for working for a cause, the cause of menstrual hygiene of the marginalised women of India. Here rings the bell – the bell of obviousness; the tale of Hema being a homemaker for 13 years because she had kids to look after, she had a family to adjust to, and so on and so forth. Yes, you thought rightfully of her situation, but what's an add-on in her journey of rising from dust? It's the fact that her husband, whose stress was one of the reasons for Hema to start FemVings, lived in a far-off land. It was only her mentor who supported her, apart from her parents, who also supported her only up to an extent. Ergo, numerous responsibilities at the home front.

13 years into homemaking, handling the family and every chore at the household front, Hema says she did not anything about business until 2 years ago. But did she not already know how to manage? It was only the motivation that she lacked to start a business of her own, which fortunately was worked upon by her mentor. He helped her identify her life's vision and mission which eventually helped

her live a life driven by purpose, a life that she finds worthy, a life that keeps her busy while doing good to society.

She frequently enough goes back to the times when her in-laws, along with her newly wedded husband, did not help her adjust, appreciate her, or even made her feel she existed for them. In those years, she lost herself, the motto of her life to do something good, to make an impact on the lives of billions. Those initially difficult times come to her as a flashback every now and then, only to act as a motivating factor to keep going ahead, without looking back.

The journey 'From I can not to I can'

Hema needed a push, a provoking factor for her to take a step towards achieving her life's goal. Her belief of 'one cannot achieve success alone, always needs a supporting hand, whether in the form of a friend or family member or anybody' came true when Mr. Ajitpal played the role of her mentor. And Hema is grateful to him, to date.

Having seen and heard stories of absurd practices in villages of India, stories of infection-led deaths due to unhygienic conditions, she wanted to provide an environment where these women could live a life in fullness, thereby uplifting the women by providing proper health and hygiene. Having faced similar infections due to the use of plastic-based sanitary napkins, she could immediately connect with the cause and work towards empowering Indian women with a healthy environment.

Not only does she believe in uplifting and empowering women by providing a noble product that is totally organic but also in creating employability opportunities for the marginalised

                                                                                    Inspiring Entrepreneurs

section of women at FemVings' manufacturing unit and under their sales and distribution channels. Her belief

> Confidence, innovation, and creativity are a woman's integral part

has led her to help women achieve social and economic independence along with providing for a sustainable future for generations to come. She also says, "A healthy woman can lead a house like a queen; an unhealthy one can wreak havoc, wo kahte hain na 'tithar-pithar ho jata hai pura ghar'".

It is usually said that there must be a man of the house to take care of the family, to provide for them, but can there be a happy family without the *Woman of the Family*? No, there cannot be. She says,

> As the saying goes 'padhega India tabhi to badhega India', our aim is to propagate 'swasth naari, shakti humari'.

Saving a human from diseases and ill health is not the job of only a doctor, a nurse, or a caretaker. Taking care starts at home, with and by family members. Hema is of the opinion that it is time the society spoke of periods or menstrual health and hygiene openly, only to save the women of rural India (which you never know could be the future of urban India!). She also says, "It is time that we all stood up and stopped the use of newspapers, sand, cloth, and whatever is available in the raunchy areas of the mainland".

> Hema visualises about providing affordable hygiene to Indian women.

She says, "Why do you think there are more than 3 UPSC toppers as women in 2023? It is only because someone, years ago, in her family (possibly even a male) broke the taboo and provided for her health and hygiene at the right time while educating her about menstruation." It is a crystal clear case of inspiration and motivation to take a step toward women's hygiene. *At last, she's the one who helps create this Srishti.*

Ab, beti bachane, padhane likhane ke saath saath, socho uske swasthya ka bhi.

Hema has always believed that it takes an equal effort by both the husband and the wife of a family to build the future they seek for themselves and their families. With this faith as a base, she has been successfully able to snowball her business

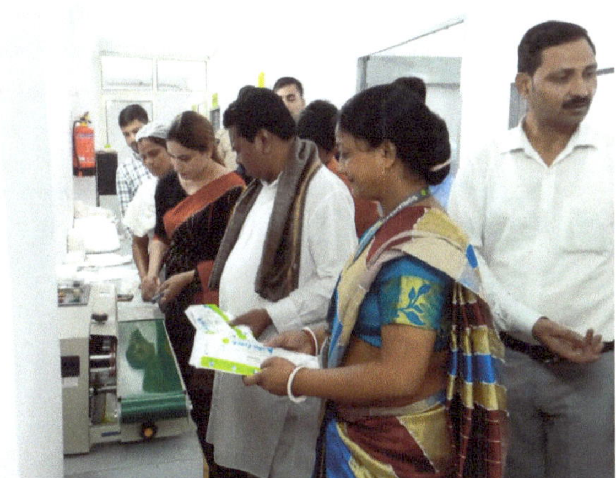

slowly while maintaining pace with her personal and social life.

The founder of FemVings, who started the organisation with 2 employees, is now working with a staff of more than 50 able women. Hema, along with her team, often enough sets up free sanitary pad distribution camps in rural parts of India. And to spread awareness about the need to start using healthier and safe options during menstruation, she arranges campaigns, seminars, and talk shows with the help of gynaecologists and other specialists.

And now that she's running her facility successfully, ministers, notable public figures, and the common man, all appreciate her, and support her, including her children. They go by her success mantra:

Jo karo pure dil se karo, junoon se karo. You will one fine day find that success. And if possible, once you're capable enough, help somebody in need and be their guiding light.

If a person has passion, one can achieve all that he/she wants. It was her passion, which is reflected even today after being successful in bringing her vision alive. Even today she fulfils all her homely duties, does not neglect her family, and takes care of her staff like another family.

RAJNI GOBHIL

Rajni Gobhil

Founder Meri Pehchan Me

> ## "Nothing in life is to be feared, it is only to be understood. Now is the time to understand more, so that we may fear less."
>
> *Marie Curie*

Rajni Gobhil, a visionary philanthropist and social entrepreneur, is on a mission to digitally empower women entrepreneurs in small businesses and is dedicated to creating an inclusive and equitable business landscape for them to thrive in the digital world.

Rajni Gobhil's journey is one of resilience, determination, and a deep commitment to community service. Born into an upper-middle-class family in Delhi, she received her education from Delhi University, where she was enrolled in a PhD programme in Operational Research. However, after getting married and moving to Gurgaon, her long commute made it impossible for her to continue her studies, and she had to drop out.

Undeterred, Rajni Gobhil used her background in Mathematics and Computer Science to work as a senior Mathematics teacher in a school. But her passion for community service soon led her to provide free Mathematics coaching to senior school

students and those preparing for competitive exams.

After a while, she resumed her career by accepting a position in a public sector organisation. After dedicating 12 years as the head of the digital data processing department, Rajni Gobhil realised that her true calling lay beyond the confines of a conventional 9 to 5 job.

Her passion for community service and empowering people propelled her to take a bold step forward and establish her own school of art in fashion. With an unwavering commitment to providing self-employable skills to women and girls, she pursued upskilling herself from NIFT Delhi in Garments Design and Retail Marketing to offer her students the best possible training.

This was just the beginning of Rajni Gobhil's journey as an independent social and community leader. She started women empowerment programmes for needy women and girls by

WEF
WOMEN ECONOMIC FORUM
ALL LADIES LEAGUE
WEF
WOMEN ECONOMIC FORUM

conducting various awareness events, thus providing them with skills, training, and support to become financially independent.

Not content with just providing training, she also connected these women with experts and organisations to provide practical experience opportunities, making them more confident to operate in the real world.

Her passion for social responsibility led her to conceptualise and implement various awareness and skill training programmes independently and with the help of other organisations having a high regard for social work. Rajni Gobhil's story is a testament to the power of determination and a deep commitment to making a positive impact on society.

As a life member of the FICCI FLO Delhi chapter women wing, she was given the power to empower aspiring women entrepreneurs in various businesses; she got the opportunity to become part of the core management team of two of its powerful women empowerment initiatives, SWAYAM and WE SKILL.

Swayam was a platform where she connected women entrepreneurs with mentors and other service providers that were required by them to start or upscale their businesses. Under the WE

SKILL initiative, she organised employable skill training for needy women and girls and aspiring entrepreneurs!

Her efforts have truly made a difference in the lives of countless women and girls, paving the way for a brighter, more empowered future for all.

Her years of selfless service to the community have forged unbreakable bonds between her and the people she serves. Her tireless dedication to helping others has earned her the trust and support of countless individuals who have benefited from her unwavering commitment to social responsibility.

The COVID-19 pandemic posed an unprecedented challenge, but her deep connections with the community and their unwavering trust in her enabled her to continue serving people even from the confines of the four walls of her home.

Despite the difficulties presented by the pandemic, she remained steadfast in her commitment to supporting those in need, offering guidance and assistance through virtual means and other innovative solutions. With her efforts,

many were able to weather the storm and emerge stronger on the other side.

The online skill training programmes she organised during the pandemic drew the attention of many trainers who came forward to support the cause. Recognising the potential for an even greater impact, she decided to bring all the trainers together on a single platform that could connect support seekers with providers and create an even larger impact.

However, when she approached various agencies to develop a website for the cause, she faced significant challenges. They demanded hefty fees and delivered a website that did not function as intended due to technical issues, leaving her disheartened.

This experience drove her to launch 'Meripehchan.Me', a social entrepreneurship project committed to the digital empowerment of women entrepreneurs in small and micro-businesses. By providing digital support, the initiative aims to help these entrepreneurs overcome the obstacles they face in the digital world and achieve greater success.

She understands the challenges faced by solo entrepreneurs with small businesses in today's digital world and seeks to address them through this initiative, where every woman entrepreneur can have a digital presence and relevant skills that enable them to stand out and grow.

Rajni Gobhil boasts an impressive academic background, holding an MPhil in Operational Research with Computer Science from the University of Delhi. She has also achieved advanced certification in Digital Marketing and Communications from MICA, specialising in the highly sought-after fields of branding and communications. Her extensive education and specialised knowledge have enabled her to be a true leader in digital entrepreneurship and empowerment.

According to Rajni Gobhil, digital revolution has highlighted the urgent need for enhanced digitalisation within economies. However, women entrepreneurs with small and micro-enterprises lack practical training and capacity development, making it difficult for them to leverage digital infrastructure for e-commerce and digital marketing.

Through her social entrepreneurship project 'MeriPehchan.ME', she is revolutionising the business landscape by providing invaluable assistance in building a powerful online web

presence and imparting training on digital marketing and branding communication skills. Her ultimate goal is to instil unwavering confidence and a strong entrepreneurial spirit in these women, enabling them to soar higher and achieve greater success.

The mission to digitally empower women filled her with a deep sense of purpose to provide a solution that was affordable, user-friendly, and empowering. She firmly believed that every woman deserves the opportunity to pursue her passions and achieve financial independence without having to make any sacrifices.

She is especially promoting visionary women entrepreneurs from small towns by offering them a free website for establishing a robust online presence, coupled with relatable training in digital marketing and branding communications.

The aim is to enable these women to showcase their talent and expertise to the world while feeling seen, validated, and confident and allowing them to amplify their message and take their enterprises to new heights.

As she looks towards the future, she is excited about the possibility of reaching thousands of women entrepreneurs by 2024 and making a difference in their lives.

Embrace your inner strength, let your light shine bright,
Stand tall, be bold, and never give up the fight.
Unleash your power, let your voice be heard,
For you are a force to be reckoned with, a warrior, and a bird.

Rajni Gobhil's work is about more than just creating successful businesses. It's about empowering women to take control of their lives, to realise their full potential, and to make a positive impact on society.

While Rajni Gobhil's social work has primarily focused on women empowerment, she has also played a pivotal role in supporting a multitude of local and global causes as the President and Project Chairperson of the Cybercity Lions Club, a chapter of the Lions Clubs International.

Rajni Gobhil's dedication to contributing to social causes and empowering women, children, and underprivileged communities has been unwavering. In addition to the above programmes, she has been involved in the following initiatives and projects aimed at creating a better world for all.

1. Saving the environment through awareness programmes on plastic eradication, distribution of cloth bags, and plantation drives;
2. Organising inter-school competitions, organising and implementing health and hygiene camps, including dental check-ups and awareness programmes for underprivileged children;
3. Contributing to other projects such as distributing stationery and winter clothing to Anganwadi kids and walking sticks to visually impaired young girls;
4. Working towards promoting micro-entrepreneurship among underprivileged women and girls by helping them form self-support groups, thereby empowering them to become financially independent and self-sufficient.

Some of her other accomplishments:

1. She has been a member of the judging panel for inter-school painting competitions organised by district child welfare, Haryana.
2. She dedicated her time to arranging workshops for children with hearing and speech impairments to teach them the valuable art of gift wrapping and presentation.
3. She has been an integral part of the managing committee for 'Swatch Toilet Abhiyaan' by an NGO. The programme was implemented in more than 1700 government primary schools in Delhi.

4. Conceptualising and Implementing the 'Swarn Akshar' initiative in seven government primary schools across Gurgaon aimed to teach underprivileged young kids to write well. Over 600 kids participated in the programme, which helped them develop a crucial skill and regain their love for handwriting, which they otherwise would not have had the opportunity to learn.

Rajni Gobhil's mission extends beyond the empowerment of women entrepreneurs; it's about creating a better future for all. Her relentless dedication and impactful work have garnered her numerous awards, mementoes, and certificates of recognition, a testament to the transformative impact she has made in her field.

Her efforts towards creating a more equitable and inclusive business landscape for all those who aspire to make a difference are truly remarkable, and her contributions to society will undoubtedly leave a lasting impact for years to come.

Phone: +919810427323
Email: rgobhil@gmail.com, contact@ meripchchan.me
Website: www.meripehchan.me
The women digital empowerment forum: https://www.Facebook.com/groups/thedigitalwaypower
FB link: https://www.facebook.com/meripehchan.me
INSTA link: https://Instagram.com/meripehchan_me

GURLEEN KHOKHAR

Gurleen Khokhar – The Passionate Survivor

Internationally Renowned Mental Health Expert CEO Dhun App Transformational Speaker Chairperson International Human Rights NGO, Director NCNB, Author Model, Former Principal

The experiences and memories of our lives
shape us into who we are

What is this life?
If it is not
As if to walk weightless
In this thin bright air
Open and lightly
Like children
You know...

Simple joys
Easily found
That resonate
Beyond all measures.
Thus are we ushered
Gently into this world
And then challenged
To find a way home again
With our hearts open,
To where heaven knows
There are pearls awaiting.
Along with the chance
Day by gleaming day
To come to realise
The more generously
We shine
The more we will
Blossom and prosper
Along a path
Where how stunning
It is to still be alive
When those
Who could never song
Suddenly can!
And as you pause
To marvel at that
Best to know all those
Who similarly bless you
In faith
Helped make it so.

> See how boundless love
> Brings time to its knees.
> A gift beyond compare.
>
> *– A poem dedicated to*
> ***Miss Gurleen by Scott Hastie***

The experiences and memories of our lives shape us into who we are. Having survived various challenges in life, Miss. Gurleen realised that true growth lies in accepting her weaknesses and strengths. Her personal transformation from being a shy, introverted child to becoming a bold woman of substance and a transformational speaker who helps people overcome their own self-limiting beliefs has made her truly climb the ladder of success higher.

Breaking the barriers of conventional stereotypes, Gurleen initiated a new paradigm enabling people to openly talk about complex issues related to mental health, sexual wellness, and the importance of living better in relationships after separation. Hoping to inspire others going through similar struggles, she penned down her own battles of the divorce in a book named *Breakdown to Wake-up*. Since then she never had to look back as she frequently was awarded and appreciated on many talking platforms that needed a voice to inspire many young girls and boys. Her journey of receiving success in being a jury member of womenovator platform also speaks about her skills and knowledge to form practical and reliable decisions based on her educational and defence background. A lady of elegance, she has been known as a charismatic personality, winning hearts by being chosen to judge many beauty pageants and also has participated in and won titles of Monsoon Queen and has always been the front runner in any open mic event in Chandigarh. Her impeccable success of enduring a divorce with an army officer made her who she

is and she calls her life a tasteful one to continue sharing her knowledge of how important it is to have one's own identity and voice being heard. Her being a defence officer's daughter and being born in National Defence Academy, Pune, it comes easy for her to have the strength and courage to be fearless and take steps for bringing a change in society. Her life has been a roller coaster journey from speaking about a battle of her own to gaining fame and name where she took a call to address anyone coming to her and using her healing practices. She became widely known for having an aura that brings relief to mentally sick souls too.

Winning awards of interiors and being the editor of her college magazines always made her win many awards. She was much spoken about in the press and she stood out to be the all-rounder everywhere. She also earned laurels for being the

चंडीगढ़ : प्रेस वार्ता-27 में फिल्म अमानत पर वार्ता करने पहुंचे एक्टर (बाएं से) संजीव अरोड़ा, नेहा पयार और धीरज कुमार।

ताकि मन रहे खूबसूरत

विदेशों की तर्ज पर अब शहर के कॉरपोरेट भी माइंड रिलैक्सेशन से जुड़े सेशन आयोजित कर रहे हैं। इसमें कर्मचारियों को तनाव से राहत देने के लिए विभिन्न तरह की गतिविधियों का आयोजन होता है।

चंडीगढ़ क्लब - 1 में आयोजित स्ट्रेस फ्री सेशन में बात करती साइकोलॉजिस्ट गुरलीन खोखर। ● जागरण

सिर्फ बातें नहीं, एक्टिविटी जरूरी है

एचआर के 3 काउंसलर व भी होती है 3

कॉमेडी एक्ट करता हूं स्टे...

चंडीगढ़ क्लब - 1 में आयोजित सेशन में हिस्सा लेती विभिन्न फील्ड से जुड़ी प्रोफेशनल्स। ● जागरण

best counsellor in an NGO named Hamari Kaksha and also won the best teacher award during her teaching time period. She has been applauded by Kiran Bedi and many esteemed souls of higher cadres. Her reputation has gained her enormous respect amongst various organisations, which makes her the chosen one in every field. One of the innumerable events she participated in is the Chandigarh blind walk event where Navjot Singh Sidhu also appreciated her efforts. Her articles on colours of love were published in the Inquisitive Magazine. Adding feathers to her cap, she has been awarded for excellence by Aesthetics International Organisation for personal development and counselling. She has been the face of Nirbhaya Jyoti National Women's Achievers excellence awards. Her live shows on Shaurya online website made her

stand up for a social cause and she spoke on child abuse and positive mindset. She has participated in awareness campaigns related to breast cancer and has been duly appreciated. Freedom from adultery or an evolution, an article in a local newspaper also featured her views as a psychologist. Her success was published in million dollar seconds book published by Brigadier Sushil Bhasin and promoted by CNBC globally. Her write-ups to advice students on competitive exams have gained importance in national newspapers. Her platform sponsored the Weaving Dreams talk organised in Chandigarh and she was also the special guest. She is passionate about time management and has written about it as well. She was awarded the Dr.S arvapalli Radhakrishnan Award on Teacher's Day. Her work and message for Little India Foundation also was spoken about a lot. She said never give up on anything which motivates the soul. She was also awarded the 100 Iconic Women Achievers Award. Her laurels also include being the international ambassador for peace and holding the title of Titanic Indian beauties by Janparishad. Her being a certified law of attraction coach also added to her educational success. She has also received the GSIL educational society's Indian Legacy Award and Aprajita Women of the Year Award. Her work as a psychologist on the need to be happy was published in Pinkishe magazine. Her seeds of educational wisdom made her start a day-care school named Windsor and she transformed many young kids to immense satisfaction. Her motto of inspiring many has always made her shift various roles in her life and she happens to be on a marathon, winning many accolades wherever she goes.

Having personally met many people from various fields and backgrounds whom she has counselled and analysed, she strongly believes in the power and importance of good and effective ways of communication. This deep insight inspired her to initiate DeepTalks – her own talk show

चंडीगढ़ : सेमिनार की आयोजक गुरलीन खोखर ●जागरण

सिटी स्पंदन

www.jagran.com

चंडीगढ़, 2 जुलाई 2019

भारत में आज भी सेक्स पर चर्चा एक टैबू है जिसपर अमूमन हम चर्चा नहीं करते। मगर सोच की उड़ान देश के नाम सेशन में इस पर खुलकर बातचीत की गई। जिसमें ट्राईसिटी के विभिन्न बुद्धिजीवियों ने हिस्सा लिया।

सोच की एक नई उड़ान

जागरण संवाददाता, चंडीगढ़ : पीढ़ियों से रिश्तों पर बातचीत होती है। मगर सेक्स ऐसा टॉपिक है जिस पर हम अक्सर अटक जाते हैं। हर पीढ़ी इस पर बात करने में असहज महसूस करती है। जिसकी वजह से वे विषय अक्सर सामने नहीं आ पाता। रिश्तों, सेक्स और अपनी पहचान पर आधारित एक सेशन का खास आयोजन शहर में हुआ। जिसमें एक नए अंदाज से चीजों को देखा गया। नई सोच की उड़ान देश के नाम पर आधारित इस सेमिनार में शहर के कई बुद्धिजीवी शामिल हुए। इस सेमिनार को आयोजन मनोवैज्ञानिक गुरलीन खोखर ने किया। इसमें डॉ. दीपक पुरी, शारदा कथापलिया वीजे अमन, जसप्रीत, धनंजय भी शामिल हुए।

खुद की पहचान को मजबूती से रखो

सेशन में धनंजय भी शामिल हुए। उन्होंने कहा कि हमें आज के समय में खुद को समझना होगा। खुद को मजबूती से सामने रखना भी जरूरी है। सेक्स ऐसा विषय है जिसमें हम अभी भी खुलकर बात नहीं करते। बल्कि इस पर खुल कर बात हो तो हम इसे नई पीढ़ी को भी बेहतर तरीके से समझा सकते हैं जिससे कि वह इसको लेकर कभी असमंजस में नहीं होंगे।

चंडीगढ़ क्लब सेक्टर–1 में आयोजित सोच की उड़ान देश के नाम सेमिनार में सोमवार को शहर की विभिन्न हस्तियों ने हिस्सा लिया ●जागरण

दिल का ख्याल ज्यादा करें

डॉ. दीपक पुरी ने कहा कि मेंटल हेल्थ बहुत जरूरी है। मैंने कितने ही केसिस देखे हैं जिसमें हार्ट फेल्योर रिश्तों में तनातनी के कारण होते हैं। हमें मेंटल हेल्थ की जरूरत को समझना होगा। हमारे रिश्ते, प्यार और सेक्स। ये ऐसे मुद्दे हैं जिसमें हमें खुलकर बोलना होगा। बातचीत बेहतर साधन है कि हम अपना तनाव एक दूसरे के साथ साझा कर सकें। दरअसल हमारा स्वास्थ्य हमारी सेक्स लाइफ से भी जुड़ा होता है। ऐसे में इसमें संकोच की जगह अपने पार्टनर से खुलकर बात करें।

मर्द व औरत के फर्क को मिटाना होगा

पंचकूला लेडीज क्लब की हेड शारदा ने कहा कि हमें समाज में मर्द और औरत के बीच के फर्क को मिटाना होगा। हमें रिश्तों और सेक्स से जुड़े मुद्दों पर बात करनी ही चाहिए। इसके अलावा स्कूल में भी सेक्स एजुकेशन को बढ़ावा देना चाहिए जिसकी वजह से हम बच्चों को गुमराह होने से बचा सकेंगे।

हमें हर पीढ़ी को साथ में लेकर चलना है

वीजे अमन ने कहा कि हमें बोल्ड टॉपिक को साझा करना ही चाहिए। इससे पीढ़ियों के बीच का अंतर भी कम होगा और हम एक–दूसरे से सहज रूप से बात भी कर सकेंगे। मॉडल जसप्रीत ने कहा कि हमें हर बोल्ड विषय पर बातचीत करना जरूरी है। हमें ज्यादा से ज्यादा सहज तरीके से इसे बाहर लाना चाहिए।

हमारा आज जरूरी है

गुरलीन ने कहा कि हम अकसर भविष्य की चिंता में आज को खराब करते हैं। या तो भूतकाल की किसी समस्या को आज तक लेकर बैठे रहते हैं। ऐसे में जरूरी है कि हम आज में जीएं। आज में जीना, हमारा आज ही नहीं बल्कि भविष्य में भी सेहत सुधारता है। हमें आज की समस्या आज ही डिस्कस करना चाहिए। इससे हम आज के साथ आने वाले कल को भी बेहतर बनाते हैं।

where she hosted innumerable enlightened souls globally who had themselves overcome limiting beliefs and shared their challenges from 'Can I' to 'I can' rise in life.

Her show Deep Talks is designed to challenge various taboos around the globe and to raise the bar of self-expression in the right manner. She wholeheartedly credits Mr. Gary Barnes, a famous American businessman, who encouraged and inspired her to pursue her passions whether it be writing or spirituality, which gave her the impetus to move ahead during her tough times of battling her dilemmas of career choice and made her look up for a way out to showcase her inner skills and abilities. She feels Mr. Gary's business mastery boot camp helped transform her into an effective talk show host and a speaker with a global standing with an edge over others in soft skills.

पीकेआर जैन वाटिका में संतुलित खानपान व व्यक्तित्व विकास के दिए टिप्स

अम्बाला सिटी | पीकेआर जैन वाटिका में मंगलवार को मासिक इग्नाइट एन इंस्पायर मोटिवेशनल टॉक कार्यक्रम के तहत बहुआयामी प्रतिभा गुरलीन खोखर ने व्यक्तित्व विकास एवं संतुलित खानपान बारे बताया। गुरलीन खोखर ने कक्षा 9वीं से 12वीं के छात्रों को सफल व्यक्ति बनने के टिप्स दिए। मौके पर प्राचार्या उमा जैन स्कूल मैनेजिंग कमेटी प्रधान धर्मपाल जैन, उप प्रधान प्रोफेसर अशोक जैन, सचिव अशोक जैन, वरुण जैन, हर्ष जैन, गौरव जैन, अमन जैन व भाविक जैन मौजूद रहे।

Being a public figure in Chandigarh, Gurleen has always aspired to work towards the growth and development of our nation. She believes that her zest for serving humanity is only heightened when she counsels people and heals souls without any expectations by the sheer investment of her time and efforts. Being an ardent Lord Shiva disciple, she also strongly believes in the power of manifestations. One of her deepest desires always made her speak about the healing powers of sex and how it relates to reduction in mental issues including improvement in relationships that have gone astray.

Gurleen had always aspired to be known as a global speaker. Another turning point in her life came when she met Michelle Mras during the most challenging times of the pandemic. Michelle invited her to her Random Shift programme and gave her a platform to speak about the importance and healing powers of a good sex life in overcoming the menace of extramarital relations and unhealthy love affairs, which often lead people to substance abuse and other dire consequences. Their show was an overnight success and the views and praise they received exceeded all their expectations. Importantly, it reinforced her belief in the importance of self-expression and the need to talk about issues that are often brushed under the carpet. Following the success of their show, Gurleen was invited to Meaningful Conversations by Beata Seweryn-Reid, where she talked about her journey and shared her experiences of being a psychologist, author, former model, and principal. Gurleen has always believed in living life to its fullest, no matter which stage and age we are in.

Gurleen's interview on Susan Kathleen's 23rd globally ranked podcast "Awakening your mind magic" further boosted her confidence and uplifted her spirits. Susan appreciated Gurleen for both her beauty and thoughts and called her an Indian version of Coco Chanel and a stylist with a taste of dressing future souls.

Gurleen feels that such accolades, particularly during the initial struggling days, go a long way in fuelling a person's thoughts and passions. Today, she is frequently invited to news channels to air her views and debate and discuss burning topics such as sex abuse, suicide, bipolar depression, mental health issues, etc. Being the daughter of a warrior, Wing Commander Bikram Dev Singh, Shaurya Chakra awardee, she feels easy to speak on mental health, freedom of speech, and human rights. She is also often invited to write articles in leading national and regional newspapers and in magazines on issues that very few dare to speak about.

Gurleen's foray into the fashion world also was admired when she served a Bollywood label named 'Zameen Asmaan-Pali's crochet work', which also helps underprivileged women. The label was one

of the chosen collections by Tarun Tahiliani and was endorsed by actresses like Kangana Ranaut, Priyanka Chopra, and Lara Dutta who was crowned in a dress of the same label. Being initially married to an Army Officer, she also got an opportunity to fulfil her modelling desires and was active in creating her own anchoring ways and fulfilled some of her passionate desires. She considers her mother Amrit Kaur, who was born in Kenya as her inspiration for maintaining an edge above others in various creative endeavours. Her sister Jasleen Khokhar has been her pillar of strength from their schooldays for navigating the ups and downs of life. She never forgets to pay her gratitude to her ancestors for passing on their skills and values and giving her the privilege to carry forward their legacy.

Gurleen launched her platform 'Soch Ki Uddan Desh Ke Naam' in 2017. This experience made her realise the skewed perceptions people have about Intelligence Quotient (IQ) and the lack of awareness about Emotional Quotient (EQ). Her views on the importance of EQ resonated well with people, and she started being called upon as a chief guest and speaker at various events in Chandigarh and the national capital. She fondly remembers when she was called upon to inspire kids of PKR Jain Vatika School in Ambala by Mrs. Uma. Several leading newspapers and news channels covered her views on the importance of motivating students and kids to remain stress-free in academics and excel in their passions and not only academics. Gurleen's life's goal is to inspire as many people as possible, and she hopes to be remembered as a generous soul who did good. Considering the materialistic lifestyle currently being adopted by people where basic human values are taking a backseat, she is working towards educating people to bring a balance between their inner and outer selves. Having judged many fashion pageants and walked the ramp as a psychologist for doctors and cardiologists of Chandigarh, Gurleen is someone who has worn many hats. She believes that it is imperative that we as humans become more comfortable in sharing our true selves, be it around our immediate relations or complete strangers since authenticity is the key to a happy and fulfilling life. To this effect, she is committed to standing strong in voicing out pertinent and bold issues that need society's attention and more than that, need a solution-centred focus for resolving grave concerns.

Being born in the National Defence Academy (NDA), Gurleen considers herself a privileged soul of a heroic father, who has served the Indian Airforce and who was awarded the Shaurya Chakra by the then president Gyani Zail Singh for saving many lives in a rescue operation in the Himalayas.

Taking forward the heroic footsteps of her family, Gurleen feels devoted and dedicated to working towards humanitarian purposes and bringing a smile to everyone. The rapidly evolving changes in our technology-driven lives have driven her to launch an application named Dhhun (www.dhunapp.com), to go back to the basics and bring back the human touch in our lives. She strongly feels that our resilience and our need for having enough patience are on a rapid decline and that people are becoming more and more isolated and irritated, leading them to commit serious crimes and activities that are not conducive to our nation. There is thus an urgent need to make people feel wanted, to have someone to hear them out. This is what Dhhun aspires to do. To explain to people the relevance of not popping pills immediately and resorting to a friendly gesture of taking the help of expert guidance is the reason why Nitin Upadhyaya, a scientist, physicist, and a mathematics professor, and she joined hands to create Dhhun.

A voice unheard is often considered dead, and the deep root causes are left unaddressed. It deeply saddens her to know how difficult it is for people to express, or even to reach out to a counsellor to overcome their challenges. The pressing concern of every household is to have someone to talk to, to be heard, looked out for, and cared for. She aspires to provide an ear to the worries of people, be they youngsters or elders. Her mental health app Dhhun, and her talk show DeepTalks is meant to provide people with the much-needed catharsis to release their pent-up emotions.

Being the chairperson of international human rights liberties and social justice, and the chairperson of Jan Parishad Women Chapter, she advocates the honest path to voicing one's concerns for the safety and wellness of all humanity. Not only this, being the Director of the National Council of News and Broadcasting, she is forever thankful to God for giving her the opportunity to reach the topmost hierarchy form where she can keep on igniting all the passionate souls walking this earth, for concerns that can uplift all of humanity.

डेमोक्रेटिक फंट (विनोद कुमार तुषावर) . चंडीगढ़ युवा दल की महिला विंग की अध्यक्ष गुरलीन खोखर को ऑल इंडिया काउंसिल ऑफ ह्यूमन राइट्स, लिबर्टीज एंड सोशल जस्टिस ने चंडीगढ़ और पंजाब की महिला चेयरपर्सन नियुक्त किया है, गुरलीन को परिषद के संस्थापक अध्यक्ष डॉ एंथनी राजू द्वारा जारी एक अधिसूचना के माध्यम से नियुक्त किया गया है, गुरलीन की क्षमता और दूरदर्शिता को देखते हुए भारतीय मानवाधिकार, स्वतंत्रता और सामाजिक न्याय परिषद ने अध्यक्ष पद के लिए उनके नाम का प्रस्ताव रखा, जिसे परिषद के संस्थापक अध्यक्ष डॉ. एंथनी राजू ने स्वीकार कर लिया, गुरलीन खोखर को चेयरमैन नियुक्त होंने पर चनडीगढ़ कांग्रेस पार्टी में खुशी की लहर दोड़ पड़ी है ।

Gurleen is not someone to rest on her laurels. Whenever she has received an achievement, she has always tried to raise the bar a notch higher. When people ask her as to what drives her to work towards her goals, she has a simple answer–"the fire in me of a passionate survivor is still dancing". A lit soul can only enlighten the souls around. The word negative connotes the darker side of humanity: a side that one must learn to accept. To achieve anything in life one has to go through a dark tunnel, and eventually come out wiser and mature and to then pass on the baton. Her ultimate aim in life is to work with public and private organisations, including politicians and celebrities with a wider reach, so as to raise awareness about mental health issues and collectively arrive at lasting solutions. Considering the current state of depression in our nation, she is on a mission to offer various options to people to deal with their personal struggles. In this light, she encourages everyone to join in their mental health app Dhhun. We all need to come together, meet and greet new people, and give everyone the opportunity to live a life of dignity and respect. She feels most passionate about mental health and has made herself a promise to reach the pinnacles one day by resolving various deep-rooted concerns of many souls.

Gurleen considers herself blessed to have someone like Dr. Moshin Walli, a Padma Shree Awardee, who has served as the physician for the president of India, and who publicly testifies to her work as a CEO, psychologist, chairperson, and director, as her constant mentor and guide. Standing for unity, love, peace, and harmony, Gurleen always goes the extra mile to support all the women and men around the globe and to encourage them to share their challenging life stories through her gmail gurleenkhokhar@gmail.com. She loves to connect with people and host them on her talk show to reignite the fire within them, and to inspire others who may be going through similar challenges. She hopes to soon publish her book that captures people's stories and journeys of overcoming their mental health challenges. The most precious gift that anyone can give to anyone else is their valuable time and attention. It would be right to mention that nobody wants a life that drains us down. Rather, all we want is a little empathy and affection, and sometimes a little nudge, that can propel us to rise higher and higher in life. Sometimes all we need is a little encouragement to aim aimlessly for gaining an edge, which can paradoxically lead us to such profound insights and innovations that can set us on a path in life that we may have never imagined. She strongly believes in and advocates the freedom to fail many times to achieve contentment and success the mere feeling of it and to erase all taboos attached to failures, including the desire to thrive for more.

A life's journey can never be fully captured in ink. A passionate life can only be lived to the very last breath. Such is Gurleen's zest for life and her passion to work towards the upliftment of mankind. Gurleen is a survivor, and a friend to millions. To everyone out there, she has only one message: "You deserve to be heard, you deserve attention. So, speak for yourself and reach out for help whenever you feel the need. nothing lasts forever, you will leave the words and actions eternally as imprints that many souls will like to follow. So don't think twice before initiating a new change.

I call myself a revolutionary soul treading the path of a voice that can be a melody to many."

SANJAY KUMAR AGARWAL

Sanjay Kumar Agarwal

Mentor, and coach Gopala NLP Master Trainer, Growth Accelerator Coach, TEDx Speaker & Author

It is not life itself that limits us, but rather our own limited beliefs, expectations, and perceptions of the choices that are available before us

Journey from a government officer to transformational corporate trainer, mentor, and coach

Sanjay Kumar Agarwal is popularly known among his fans and followers across the globe as a growth accelerator coach, TEDx speaker, corporate trainer, GOPTA NLP master trainer, best-selling author of 4 books, and founder of the learning movement.

Sanjay Kumar Agarwal believes that everyone has more potential than he has unlocked so far and there is a gap between where one ought to be and where he is today. He helps people to bridge this gap by working on their goals, and time utilisation patterns, and enriching and influencing communications and belief systems.

Born in Lucknow in 1967, he pursued his post-graduation in Commerce from Lucknow University. After completion of his academics, he joined the Customs & Central Excise Department where he served for 25+ years before taking VRS to follow his passion to help people grow in their personal and professional lives.

His parents were religious and the atmosphere at home gave him very strong feelings of connectedness with the Almighty God and the universe. He believes that whenever he needs something, the universe presents it in one way or the other. His wife Priti Agarwal, daughters Taru and Harshi and his elder brother Ajai Agarwal are his biggest support systems.

Journey as a professional mentor and coach

Sanjay worked for the Government of India in the Ministry of Finance for more than 25 years and took voluntary retirement in 2016 under the age of 50 to follow his purpose in life and passion for working upon the mindsets of people and helping them grow in their personal and professional lives with full focus, even though it meant letting go of a handsome salary, job security, and immense power and entering into a whole new world of professional training and mentoring, starting from scratch. Since then, he has helped countless people, entrepreneurs, and organisations to accelerate their growth rate.

After turning professional mentor and coach, the initial journey was tough. In his initial days, he had to go and speak for organisations or educational institutes that invited him, at times, even complimentary without any free choice in the matter. Today, he is an internationally acclaimed corporate trainer and speaker. He spoke at the International NLP Conference in June 2021. Connecting with global top trainers gave him the idea to organise 'International NLP Confex for Business Excellence', which was the first of its kind in the world where 28 top-notch NLP Trainers from 11 countries across the globe addressed the participants from 37 countries as to how they can unlock their business excellence. These two events brought him on the world map of acclaimed trainers in the arena of transformational mentoring and coaching.

Today, he has 4 books in his name, all published by one of the largest publishers in India, Prabhat Prakashan. He has authored the best-selling books titled 'How to Add 1000 Productive Hours A Year to Your Life', 'Sleep – It's Body Repair Time', 'Murder Procrastination', and 'Teachers are Shapers'.

He is passionate about helping people accelerate their growth and unlock their inner excellence so that they realise their true potential and achieve exponential growth in whatever field they are in.

He is the creator of his trademark concept 'GOPTA' and he has done a fusion of GOPTA with NLP and Communicative Intelligence under the brand name 'GOPTA NLP Framework'. He is the founder of the International GOPTA NLP Academy (IGNA).

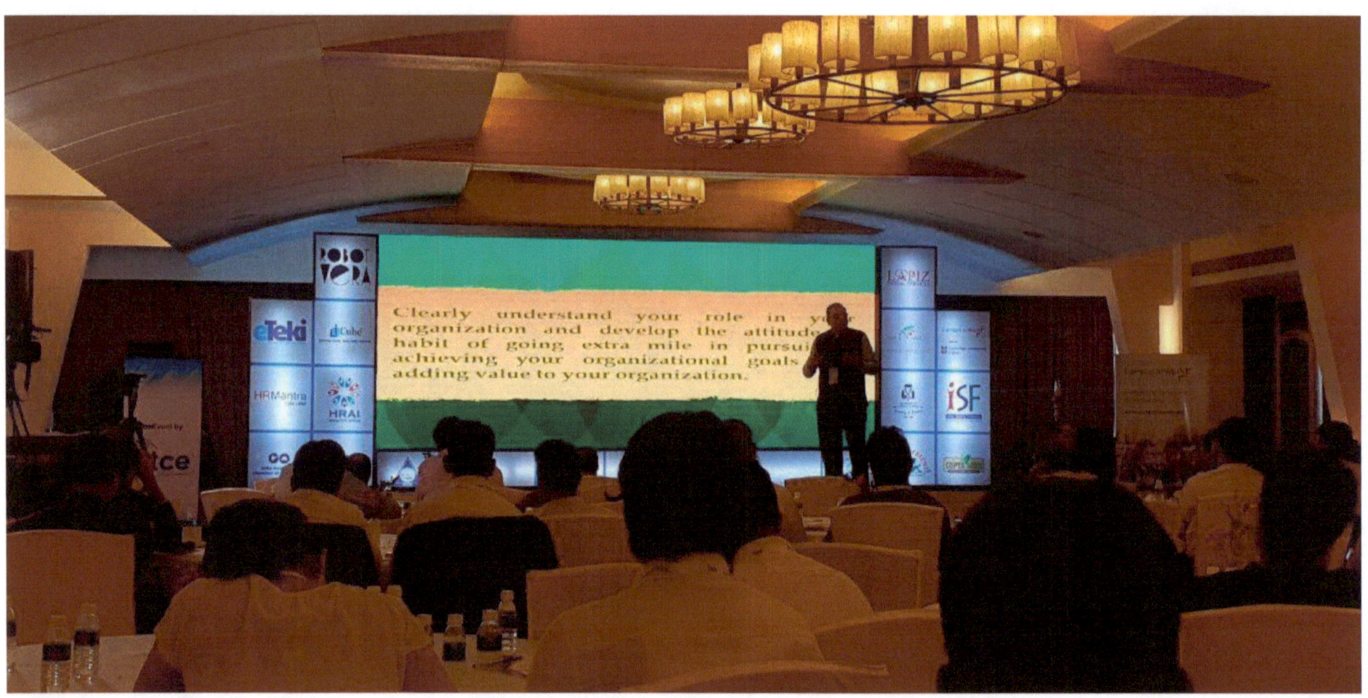

Clearly understand your role in y
organization and develop the attitud
habit of going extra mile in pursui
achieving your organizational goals
adding value to your organization.
eTeki
HRMantra
HRAI
LAPIZ
iSF

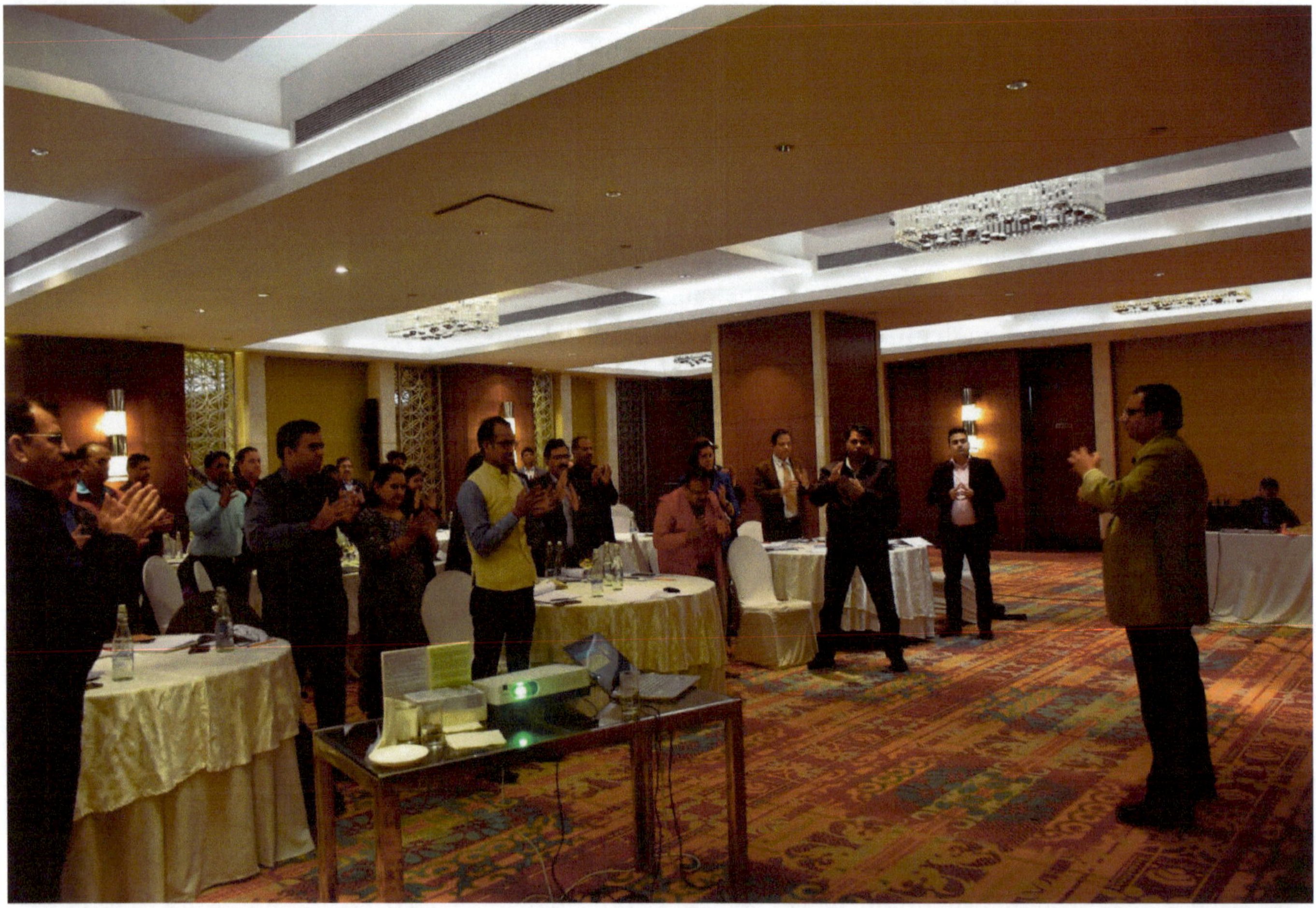

He is also the founder of 'The Learning Movement', where his mission is to inculcate the habit of 'lifelong learning' to people so that they work upon their mindset and stay ahead of the competition and achieve success in their dreams. The Learning Movement brings free learning from him as well as other trainers from across the globe along with various premium programmes, which can be bought for a better understanding of life-changing and basic concepts like goals, time management, communications, beliefs, and various other topics of importance.

His signature workshops, 'Grow with Goals', 'Murder Procrastination', 'Enhance Your Productivity', '4 Pillars of Exponential Growth', 'Influencing Communications' and many more help people to grow at a faster pace towards their goals. His signature workshop 'Relationship Mastery' is especially popular among working women and couples as he guides very deeply to maintain balance among different walks of life by improving relationships and having better control on emotions.

On being asked what is GOPTA, Sanjay reveals the secret behind GOPTA. G.O.P.T.A.® is an acronym given by him to 'Goals Oriented Positive Thinking and Actions'. Since childhood, he was passionate about learning the secrets of success and personal growth. He used to wonder how is it that some people get huge success in life while others live a mediocre life. While studying success from various sources, he learnt many ingredients of success, out of which he personally identified 3 ingredients on which you can't afford to be even 99% if you want to achieve huge success in life.

For the sake of easiness in remembering these 3 ingredients, he created an acronym and that acronym is G.O.P.T.A. which means 'Goals Oriented Positive Thinking & Actions'. He says that if one is goals oriented, his every thought, every action and time utilisation pattern will be in the direction of achieving his goals; he will inculcate the habit of asking himself, 'Whatever I am doing right now is the most appropriate usage of my time or not'. If he possesses 'positive thinking', he will impregnate his subconscious mind with positive beliefs and positive attitude and inculcate positive values and habits to speed up the journey towards his goals. He will guard his self-image from the leg-pulling and negative comments of others and will not allow others to tell him what he is capable of doing and what not. His definition of 'actions' is to take action upon oneself, that is, learning goals-oriented skills, inculcating goals-oriented habits, inculcating goals-oriented values, practicing goals-oriented time utilisation patterns, and building goals-oriented relationships.

He always says that having a GOPTA mindset is **essential** for success. If a person wants success in life, he can't afford to ignore any of the above three limbs of GOPTA.

He has done a fusion of GOPTA with the concepts of Neuro Linguistic Programming (NLP) and with various other communicative intelligence modalities provided by researchers over a period of time and created a completely wonderful growth model 'GOPTA NLP Framework'. While GOPTA provides the thought process of remaining goals oriented and possessing a positive outlook while taking persistent actions towards the goals, NLP equips a person with methodologies and

techniques to enhance the speed of his journey towards his desired outcomes.

Talking about how GOPTA NLP can solve the challenges faced by humans in general, Sanjay reveals that the sole motive behind whatever he does today is to empower people to grow in their personal and professional lives by working on all crucial facets of their life. He believes that there are 4 major pillars of exponential growth for anyone, whether he is in a job or in business or any profession:-

1. Having clear goals and strategies to achieve those goals.
2. Effective time utilisation skills.
3. Enriching and influencing communications.
4. Resourceful and empowering values and belief systems.

He believes that poor communication skills are the biggest cause of spoiled interpersonal relationships, whether in personal or professional lives. We all want to guide the conversations to our advantage, though most people are not able to make their words properly impact the mind of the other person. Similarly, we must have clearly defined goals (well-formed outcomes) and a strategy to achieve them. And in the process, we have to effectively utilise our time towards achieving those goals.

If we are able to manage all these 4 pillars of exponential growth while maintaining balance among different walks of life, this growth and success turn into inner happiness and joy.

When it comes to growth, happiness and joy, he thinks globally. He says, 'Why should this ultimate growth model remain restricted to India only'? He has founded International GOPTA NLP Academy with the mission of spreading the 'GOPTA NLP Framework' across the globe. From 2024, he will also offer franchisee of this unique concept so that trainers from across the world can come to India to learn this unique concept and enable their countrymen with this growth model under certification from International GOPTA NLP Academy.

Journey from the security of a central government job to following passion and purpose

Sanjay says that one has to follow his passion and life mission. He was doing well in his job and won many awards and rewards, still, he used to feel as if he was not contributing to the lives of others. He says that one has to take calculated risks.

His journey of transformation started in the year 2006 when he read a quote by Zig Ziglar: 'If you help enough other people to achieve what they want to achieve, you will achieve what you want to achieve'. It was the biggest turning point in his thought process. He started thinking about what he could do to help people at large and then the GOPTA framework came into his mind. Since the beginning, he knew that he had to follow something which was most close to his heart and he followed that.

He decided to work on these areas. First, he researched and researched some more before finally creating a fusion of his trademark concept GOPTA with the time-tested concepts

of Neuro Linguistic Programming (NLP) and Communicative Intelligence and formed this ultimate growth model, 'GOPTA NLP Framework'.

As we all know, every success story has at least 5 years of dedicated passionate work behind it. He has worked passionately for 20 years already. Obviously, the journey was not as simple as it looks now. No doubt, there were lessons to be learnt. He took those lessons and worked on his marketing skills. He worked on building a strong foundation in this new area of life. He created the spiral of trust by delivering value to his participants who gradually became his main source of referrals and brought new participants to his workshops. To summarise, huge success is never an overnight process, though it seems to be.

He loves nurturing relationships based on mutual trust and win-win for both. Many professional relationships go far beyond professional training and they start growing together as they understand the needs of each other. His core area is to make people identify their core strengths and work around those core strengths. It works wonders for them.

By understanding the thinking behind all behaviour, one can gain insight into how beliefs, values, habitual structures, and perceptions of life can have positive or negative influences on how one chooses to interact with the world and the effect they have on it and vice versa.

It is not life itself that limits us, but rather our own limited beliefs, expectations, and perceptions of the choices that are available before us. And with this unique GOPTA NLP Framework, one can overcome all these challenges and join the community of a few people who are living a truly successful life with a sense of fulfilment.

He believes that success without maintaining a reasonable balance among different walks of life and without a sense of fulfilment and staying an underperformer in comparison to his own true potential is the BIGGEST failure!

His books are available at Amazon at bit.ly/BooksBySanjay.

To know more about him and his work, you may visit linktr.ee/sanjaykumaragarwal or scan the QR Code.

ADITI HANDA

Aditi Handa

Co Founder & Head Chef the Bakers Dozen

These two entrepreneurs... are toast!

Life partners and the founding duo of TBD, Sneh and Aditi crossed paths in 2008 when Sneh was still in his 2nd year of MBA and Aditi was on a break, while studying Psychology in England. Aditi dreamt of finding innovative ways of serving the nation like her freedom-fighter grandparents, whereas Sneh wanted to channel his inner risk-taking Marwari genes to start a business while Indian entrepreneurs were on the global map. Their love story began while they accidentally broke bread together (quite literally) at IIM A since Aditi's father was also Sneh's professor of entrepreneurship (yes, yes, there's a whole DDLJ story right there – but that's for when we loaf around some other time). TBD was thus truly a labour of love, with a duo connecting over a common love and enthusiasm for entrepreneurship.

The 'Knead' to Rise

It was Feb 2012 by the time Aditi and Sneh were married and settled in Canada when the entrepreneurial bug really bit. Sneh decided to finish his last project with McKinsey and Co. and the couple, along with Aditi's younger brother Siddharth, considered joining hands to establish a business. The trio started broadening their thoughts by discussing various business ideas, ranging from common goals such as setting up a factory to esoteric stem cell research, etc., and even visiting multiple trade fairs to understand the fundamentals of building a substantial brand.

Baking the Business Idea

How do you spot a radical baker?
They're always going against the grain.

In the latter half of 2012, during one of their visits to Bombay, Aditi Handa and Sneh Jain came across an observation made by a friend 'India mein achi bread nahi milti' (We don't get good bread in India). At that time, the couple dismissed this as a passing observation until one day Aditi's mom expressed the same concern. The Handa household always served entrepreneurial conversations on the dinner table, and this lament stuck with the duo, who began to mull over this apparent gap for good varieties of bread in the Indian bread industry.

Incidentally, before she visited India, Aditi had interned with a Lebanese chef in a small restaurant in Toronto – an experience she enjoyed tremendously – and working in the food industry thus became the first substantial idea they sealed on. A few interesting ones from the list were to introduce an online grocery store like Big Basket, an old age home, or to start something in the healthcare sector/pharma business. Eventually, the final idea was to establish a bakery business in India and serve the country with premium baked products. Particularly about cementing her technical expertise and predisposition to culinary arts, Aditi decided to go to the French Culinary Institute in New York to learn how to bake. It was during this period that they decided to start their journey with bread, specialising in sourdough.

Well-bread – Onto becoming the Knightin-Dough of the country

In April 2012, while Aditi was learning to shape one of her first sourdoughs (a French Pain Aux Cereales) at the French Culinary Institute New York, she felt a love for baking like never before. Shaping and baking a sourdough felt sacred to her, and she transcended to a deeply spiritual place by intuitively chanting the Gayatri Mantra as she laminated her first croissant sheet, to make sure her turns were perfect.

From mixing to shaping the dough of the bread, Aditi felt an unimaginable passion for the process of baking. She decided that she would be honest

across all walks of life – be it while baking bread or running a business – one of the key ingredients for TBD's success even today.

While Aditi was being trained under some of the best chefs who helped her pillar her enthusiasm to build a brand, her co-founder and husband Sneh Jain was on the lookout for kitchens in Mumbai to realise this 'well-bread' dream. Ultimately, the same year, The Baker's Dozen began its journey via a small kitchen and 4 bakers in Mumbai.

A Platter of Dreamy Bakes for the Country

The Entry Of Sourdough into the Indian Household

Sourdough or preferment, as it is technically known, is one of the world's oldest traditions in bread making, vivacious and diverse from region to region. While the Europeans ferment flour and water and use it to leaven the dough, some Middle-Eastern regions use fermented chickpea water to leaven their flatbreads.

From having baked her first batch to now running a decade-old thriving business, Aditi and her understanding of this flavourful and humble bread have indeed come a long way.

When Handa-Jain started the brand, they made their own starter to ferment the bread, calling it the mothership sourdough for TBD, which would help create new, fresh sourdough breads every day. They wanted to source all ingredients locally but faced their biggest challenge – Indian flour was weak by nature when it came to working with the sourdough technique and incapable of developing a strong structure by itself. The couple also wanted to ensure that they made an 'All-Indian' bread, with accrued benefits of health and taste for every Indian household.

Much like a scientist in her private lab of experiments, Aditi found herself dwelling more and more into this mystery – be it in her factory or her home kitchen. After much Research and Development, she was able to find the right ingredients for her starter's secret sauce,

ensuring a 100% whole wheat sourdough loaf that was naturally capable of increased shelf life while providing fantastic benefits for the gut.

And the same starter is used for fermenting TBD breads even today.

Such is the power of TBD's delicious Sourdough starter that the bread, even if it dries up, returns to

Banana Walnut and Orange Cake (From left to right) by Aditi Handa

its normal texture by simply toasting it to the right temperature. Can your average Joe of sliced bread compete with that?

Contributing to Healthier Living

Made with love, TBD bakers use a generous amount of seeds in their bread. For every 100 gm of flour, they add 64 gm of seeds – more abundant than any other bread in India! Quality comes at a price, but not to the end consumer in TBD's case. Unlike its competitors who often skim off the good stuff, TBD uses only top-notch varieties of high-end pumpkin and sunflower seeds (that are 8–10 times more expensive than others) in an equal proportion to sesame and flax, so that the end product is delicious and tasty while being pocket-friendly.

Keeping it local and natural is the brand's motto, as an orange cake is made from cold-pressed orange juice, which is 100% orange juice. The banana walnut cakes are made from fresh bananas devoid of any essences. TBD only uses fresh yeast

TBD bakes 100% whole wheat breads that are also naturally richer in protein

since they use a high-protein flour to avoid adding flour enhancers.

or preferment/sourdough because the fresher the fermenter the better and more alive the product is.

What's great about TBD's bread (story)? It never gets stale. (aka Did you know?)

It took TBD over a year to come up with a preservative-free, stabiliser-free eggless cake!

It took TBD over 3 years to come up with a gluten-free range that not only is healthy but really really tasty!

TBD is the first bakery in India to commercialise sourdough breads with these many different flavours.

Even basic products like pav, pizza bases, and sliced sandwich bread are all made with the goodness of sourdough!

The seeds in four grains are 65% in ratio to the flour, and yes all the seeds are equally distributed. The expensive ones are not less in ratio. It took them 6 months of trials to make 100% whole wheat breads and cakes, even the starter is whole wheat.

Ciabatta is their most hydrated i.e., 80%, elongated, broad, and flatbread famous for its unique alveolar holes

Brioche is loaded with pure butter, in fact, 60% of butter.

Laminating the dough 25 times a day is the secret behind their mouth-melting croissant

TBD loves the concept of farm to fork, so they started applying this by using ingredients from their own farm :
Fresh lemon for their lemon loaf.
Freshly grated carrots for carrot walnut cake.
Cherry tomato and capsicum for focaccia.

TBD dark chocolate cookies contain the same ratio of dark chocolate and flour **and** Cashew cookies **are loaded with cashews. They contain** 45% of cashew in it.

The Decadent Journey – Stuffed with Pride, Sprinkled with Joy.

Enlightening the audience: Upon launch, the brand acknowledged that its biggest challenge was customer awareness regarding the sourdough technique, making these hand-shaped crusty loaves seem foreign and quite daunting at first sight. Thus, the founder duo ensured they invested their time and efforts in helping their customers to better understand the sourdough itself, before marketing their own brand. Both Aditi and Sneh would spend 12-hour days at their stores, interacting with their customers and educating them on the nutritious benefits of sourdough for daily consumption. Today, these endeavours have led to TBD's ride to an iconic bakery brand that has not only introduced Indians to these gut-friendly breads but also enlightened them with the 'how to fit' and 'how to eat' aspects, making it a regular in the Indian household pantry.

Customer Centricity: Since its inception, TBD has always been a customer-centric brand. The mindset shift of the Indian customer towards conscious foods and mindful eating has led to a surge in demand and curiosity for TBD's authentic breads. Each feedback by a customer through any channel is read by at least one founder personally to further understand their needs and then develop new lines basis their lifestyle requirements.

Redefining the bakery industry: In India, consumers can buy bread and other bakes only on the basis of their suggested softness and freshness. The Baker's Dozen is amongst one of the very few digital-first bakery brands who with its D2C business model, massive reach, and strong distribution channel offers high-quality artisan bakes to anyone and anywhere without them having to step out or burning a hole in their pocket. It has also changed the perception of the Indian bakery industry, which was earlier recalled as a

semi-organised sector with a lack of technology and hygiene practices. The Baker's Dozen, as one of the largest artisan bakery brands, stands out with its streamlined sanitation and hygiene design in its 25,000 sq. ft factory, also the first pandemic-ready production plant in the country.

Bringing Sourdough Into The Mainstream: Striving hard to blend customer centricity with an efficient and strong distribution channel, The Baker's Dozen is one of the largest artisan brands that makes sourdough available to almost every corner of the country. The brand also spends a great amount of time and energy spreading awareness about how sourdough is a much healthier option than commercial bread and to break its perception as gourmet food, but more as a bread that brings extra oomph and nutrition to the everyday breakfast plate.

Rising up against the Pastry-archy / TBD's Uppercrust – How the Amateur Baked Success to Perfection

When Aditi first decided to train as a baker, she enrolled in a well-renowned institute in Bangalore, only to quickly realise that she would not learn the right skills in India, since they didn't pay any heed to the importance of technique at all. She knew, then, that she had to choose a dedicated bread-baking programme, which led her to join The International Culinary Centre in New York.

During this period, her passion for baking grew manifold. However, on returning to India, she didn't find the same passion in any other chef she met. Disillusioned with the existing baking talent, Aditi decided to build the world's most-loved bakery brand – while scouting inclusive and diverse talent for her kitchen!

"I may not have had as much experience and knowledge as my chefs/teachers did, but they had imbibed in me a passion and honesty towards my product. I knew that was going to be enough. There were many people out there who actually wanted to learn something and had the passion to adopt the technique. I started training the people on the basis of their interests irrespective of their qualifications and background. They have proved to be the best team I would ever have."

> "Someday, I would like The Baker's Dozen to be not just known for the best sourdough but also the best training ground for young, enthusiastic people who otherwise wouldn't have received this opportunity."
>
> – Aditi Handa

Today, the brand is recognised as one of the strongest brands in the bakery category for both retail partners such as Nature's Basket and also new-age e-commerce partners such as Swiggy, Zomato, Swiggy Instamart, Big Basket, MilkBasket, SuprDaily, etc.

How does TBD remember its milestones? It uses Toast-It notes

2013	Setup 1000 sq. ft. kitchen in Mumbai; commercially launched with their first standalone store in Prabhadevi
2014–15	Opened 7 standalone stores across Mumbai
2016–17	Moved to 5000 sq. ft. kitchen in Navi Mumbai Expanded to modern trade retail formats across Mumbai and Pune
2017–18	Expanded to Bangalore and Ahmedabad through modern trade partnerships

2019	Commissioned a new 25,000 sq. ft. factory near Ahmedabad and became the first Indian bakery to implement innovative German technology to enhance shelf life from 2 days to 10 days in breads and from 3 days to 25–30 days for sponge cakes. Monthly production capacity grew by 2.5× in the last 3 months itself to cater to the growing demand – from 60 tons in October 2021 to around 150 tons in December 2021
2020	Selling a million sourdough loaves across India Being pioneered one as India's first COVID and similar pandemic-ready 25000 sq. ft baking factory alongside other innovations in 2020 Well-thought expansion – To open 50 outlets across 15 cities by the end of 2021
2021	3 walk-in stores and 18 delivery-only outlets (across the country) One of the strongest brands in the bakery category for both retail partners such as Nature's Basket and also new-age e-commerce partners such as Swiggy, Zomato, Swiggy Instamart, Big Basket, MilkBasket, SuprDaily etc.

I hear sourdough is on the rise

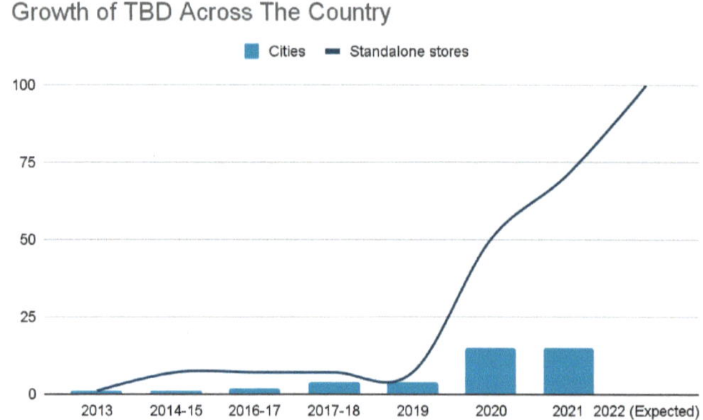

The Baker's Dozen is currently at an ***ARR of INR 40 cr growing at a phenomenal growth rate of more than 500% over the last 2 years!*** (OR experiencing phenomenal 5× growth over the last 2 years). TBD today is a preferred brand of choice and has so far won the hearts of 50,000 customers across more than 20 cities in India.

Moreover, the COVID-19 pandemic accelerated its growth, and in 2020, TBD achieved the milestone of selling a million sourdough loaves across India, followed by announcing their major offline expansion plans and strengthening their digital presence with their own app. At the same time, their digital campaign 'The Dose We Knead' to support the government's vaccination drive observed huge success with 10000+ registrations within a short span of 15 days.

In addition to growing on different channels, TBD's team and consumer base also evolved simultaneously. TBD now has a team of 350 members pan-India from Dec '21—a massive 3× jump compared to pre-COVID levels and is further estimated to reach 500 by the end of 2022.

What are the chances of finding a better sourdough in India? Naan-existent

- ➢ The only brand to offer preservative-free and high-quality breads in India at an affordable range starting from Rs. 50 using unique FreshLock packaging technology.
- ➢ It is one of the strongest brands in the bakery category on Swiggy, Zomato, Swiggy Instamart, Big Basket, MilkBasket, SuprDaily etc.
- ➢ The largest bakery supplier to Nature's Basket stores pan-India and chains such as Foodhall, Star Bazaar etc.

- The only bakery brand in India to use the innovative Freshlock Packaging to increase the shelf life of its products without adding any preservatives; also making the product the most hygienic available!
- The first bakery brand to develop a new-age feature-packed website and app with options for subscriptions etc.; also developed bots for Whatsapp ordering.
- A rare bakery company to use AI- and ML-backed data science software to estimate demand, ensuring availability while minimising wastage.

From SourDOUGH to SourBRO:

Truly premium in every aspect: By virtue, handmade and artisanal products are more difficult and time-consuming to make. Getting the consistency and accuracy similar to a machine-made product is difficult. When one chooses to make a handmade product, it is to keep the art alive; the motives are very rarely commercial. When a product is artisanal, it does not have any harmful artificial ingredients such as preservatives or chemicals. The goodness of the ingredients is preserved during the manufacturing process by not subjecting them to hard machine-based processes. The manufacturing cost of artisanal products is generally higher than most machine-made mass products.

TBD has always believed in using local produce to build an honesty-driven, high-quality and delicious product that stays true to its technical expertise while keeping the price of the product affordable and always available to any person who chooses to adopt it into their lifestyle.

Baking innovation: TBD has always believed in continuous innovation when it comes to developing a product. Two years ago, TBD converted most of its products, including cakes, to 100% whole-wheat. They also launched a range called 'Fit Kneads' which has gluten-free and high-protein products. These are designed not just to be healthy but very tasty.

Leavening outreach: In 2020, the brand embarked upon a journey to be India's largest D2C artisan bakery, requiring them to level up in every possible way. They had to become more accessible to the community, ensuring absolute ease in the order process of a customer's favourite products, while amplifying the love they have showered on TBD since the beginning. So, they decided to focus on the digitisation of the business. This included building a new website and App (Android as well as iOS) with an intuitive UI with specialised features for maximum conversions.

In 2022, the brand was also working on developing machine learning data science modules to reduce wastage, strengthen the end-to-end supply chain, and reduce the frequency and intensity of customer dissatisfaction cases. The company also believes in making decisions based on true analytical data and predictive analysis inspired by the variations in the market trends to create highly customised, innovative and award-winning marketing campaigns.

Goodness packed: The company has invested in a German packaging technology that helps them naturally increase shelf life without the use of any preservatives. This technique ensures the product is packed in an inert atmosphere preventing microbial contamination, making TBD bread the most hygienic baked product in the market!

Looking towards a future well baked

- With the aim of marking 170 crore revenue by FY24, and making The Baker's Dozen India's fastest-growing D2C bakery brand, this year, the company will look at expanding to 100 brand stories and 1000 retail touchpoints across 25 cities in India, followed by strengthening its consumer base in Tier-I & Tier-II cities, and building its presence in the international market starting with Dubai and Singapore.

- The brand further plans to double its marketing spends focusing on a combination of ATL avenues such as hoardings with new-age media like influencer marketing and digital marketing. They will also be focusing on point-of-sale marketing through retail merchandise and banners/offers on e-commerce partners.

JAIPARKASH SHARMA

Jaiparkash Sharma

Differently Abled Social Activist, Motivational Speaker Certified Changemaker By Govt of India, Prop. Dadhich Stone & Deedwania Udhyog RIICO

Making Consistent Efforts is More Important Than Thinking Whether We Will Succeed or Not

This is an inspiring story of Mr. Jaiprakash, a social worker who himself is handicapped but works tirelessly for the welfare of people who are bedridden, like patients with muscular dystrophy, spinal cord injury, or polio paralysis. The story of Mr. Jaiprakash is very inspiring and motivating.

Mr. Jaiprakash has been in the field of social work for the last 25 years. Till the age of 10, he was a very healthy child and also learnt cycling. Then one day, on 31 October 1984, he suffered a polio attack. It was the day Prime Minister Mrs. Indira Gandhi was assassinated. His limbs, both legs and arms, as well as the spine stopped working. Mr. Jaiprakash's father took him to various places for treatment, even Mumbai. His elder brother, Mr. Nityanand, carried him on his shoulders to Mumbai. He was treated by Dr. GS Chawla, the biggest orthopaedic doctor in Mumbai, along with Dr. KD Dholakia from the USA. They operated on him in Mumbai and he stayed in the hospital for one year. His father had to sell two mines and a plot in Jaipur to provide Jaiprakash with the best treatment. It was not easy for the family to afford treatment for one year in a Mumbai hospital where his father and brother stayed with him. His elder brother helped him a lot. Thereafter, he stayed with his sister for two years in Hyderabad where his brother-in-law Mr. Om Prakash supported him. Then Jaiprakash started physiotherapy and through exercise, he brought improvement in his body. The way he used his willpower to exercise physically and mentally to improve the mobility of his body is remarkable, and now he is motivating other handicapped persons so that they too get the right direction like him and become self-sufficient and also create an identity for themselves in society. Mr. Jaiprakash says that he always tries to help handicapped people to bring improvement in their lives. He neither has any organisation nor is he part of any social organisation. In fact, he has a small marble business in Jodhpur, established for him by his father.

He runs programmes for handicapped persons with the help of the local administration. His business is in Mandor, Fissure Jodhpur and from his personal earnings he spends a part on the welfare of handicapped people.

Mr. Jaiprakash is the youngest of six siblings: one brother and four sisters. His business, named M/S Dadheech Stone and Didvania Udyog, deals in marble mining work which is pretty hard work, but he doesn't think of difficulties. His father Late Sh. Satyanarayan Sharma was a social worker and a good friend of the Honourable chief minister of Rajasthan Mr. Ashok Gehlot, who visited his home in 2010 when his father expired. Jaiprakash's mother Smt. Prem Kanwar was a religious and

SHEconnects
WOMEN OF SUBSTANCE
TM
HEconnects
TM
Talented Menpreneurs Network
CERTIFICATE
of Participation
Jaiprakash Sharma
Business Man & Social Worker
Delicious
Delicacies &

OUR PARTNERS
OUR PARTNERS
SMEBIZZ
CEO
STAR AWARD

social lady who passed away in 2022. His mother was always worried about him and in her last days, she trained him to do all his daily chores himself so that he becomes self-dependent and overcomes everyday challenges. She taught him to cook, clean the house, and look after himself. Jaiprakash is a teetotaller who has no vices; he never drinks alcohol, doesn't smoke and doesn't eat paan also. He eats simple meals.

His father sent him and his brother to Mumbai for the treatment of Jaiprakash. After one year, both the brothers started the business of wholesale clothes and for the next 10 years, they pursued it. In 1999, Jaiprakash came back to Jodhpur and started the business of marble and devoted his life to this work. Along with the business, he started doing social work as he was inspired by his father. In fact, he had started handicapped social service in 1994, the time he was in Mumbai.

He faced many ups and downs in social work and many times he sat for peaceful protests, often being lathi-charged by the police. He personally believes that making consistent efforts is more important than thinking only about whether we will succeed or not. He keeps writing to and meeting with administrative authorities, informing them about the problems faced by handicapped persons and seeking help. He tries to meet politicians and ministers of various states to talk about the welfare of other handicapped people. It is difficult for

him to travel due to his polio, and at times he gets physically hurt as well.

Once on 12 December 2012, when he was visiting Mahapaur for some social work, he lost his balance and injured his leg, which took 3 years for him to recover. Mr. Jaiprakash's spirits have never been defeated. Once, his operation was done incorrectly, but instead of fighting, he forgave the doctor. Jaiprakash believes that karma is supreme and it was his destiny to face this karma. He says, 'forgiveness is life, forgiving is moksha and forgiveness is happiness and dharma'.

The concept of karma was taught to him by his grandfather, Sh. Sewanand, or Sh. Radhakrishna who was a saint. Mr. Jaiprakash's great-great-grandfather was a businessman, great-grandfather was also a businessman and his grandfather became a sadhu, who took sanyas after 3 years of marriage. His grandfather had a big place in Jodhpur, which is famous by the name Gufa. His grandfather believed and prayed to God Shanker. Jaiprakash's father was a businessman and a worker of the Congress Party. Mr. Jaiprakash has many friends who are his guides also and keep guiding him from time to time. He enjoys doing business and is very happy with his work and is enjoying it.

He believes that hard work is best and one who does work hard is happy. He insists that since his mother taught him everything before

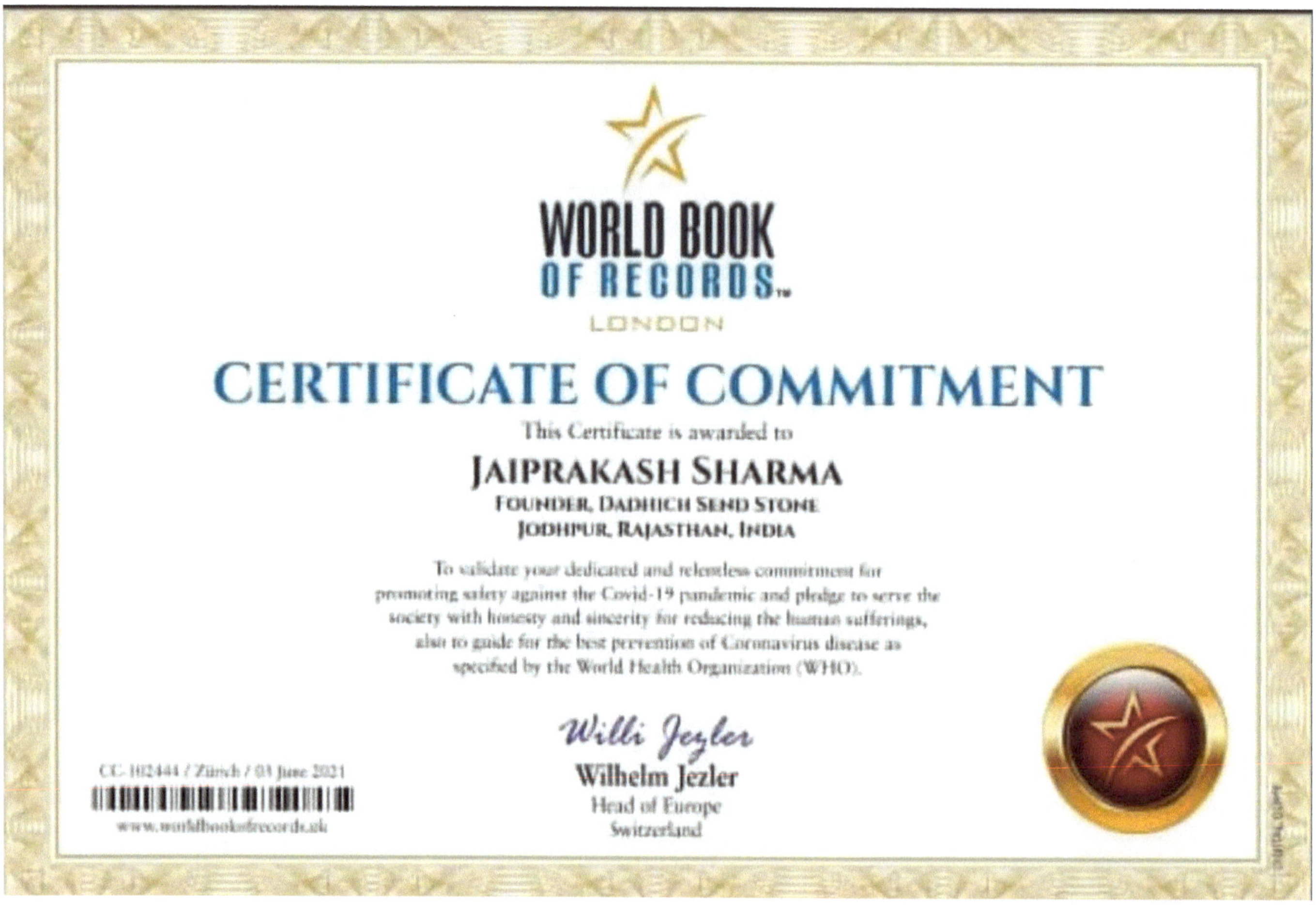

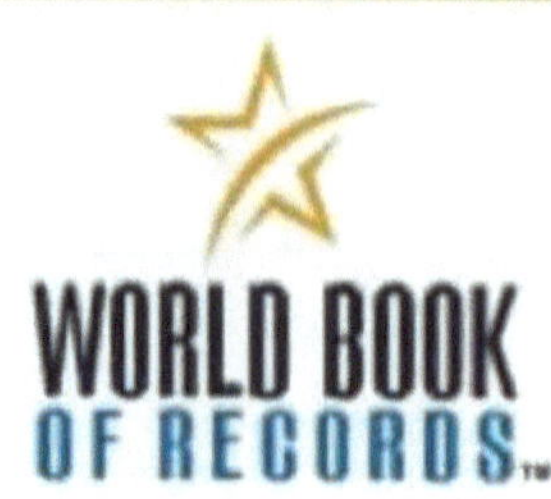

WORLD BOOK
OF RECORDS™
LONDON
CERTIFICATE OF COMMITMENT
This Certificate is awarded to
JAIPRAKASH SHARMA
FOUNDER, DADHICH SEND STONE
JODHPUR, RAJASTHAN, INDIA
To validate your dedicated and relentless commitment for
promoting safety against the Covid-19 pandemic and pledge to serve the
society with honesty and sincerity for reducing the human sufferings,
also to guide for the best prevention of Coronavirus disease as
specified by the World Health Organization (WHO).
Willi Jezler
Wilhelm Jezler
Head of Europe
Switzerland
CC-102444 / Zürich / 03 June 2021
www.worldbookofrecords.uk

she passed away, he is independent today. He motivates other handicapped people to be independent and holds many camps to help them become empowered. He says that he neither clicks pictures of handicapped persons nor allows anyone else to do it because they don't need sympathy or pity from anyone. He is known to many senior officers and they also help him in his programmes. He encountered polio at the age of 10 when he was in fifth class, and thereafter he spent time in exercises to improve his body. He could not complete his 10th as he did not get time for study owing to the fact that he faced many physical challenges. As time passed, he met many good people in life who helped him and became his friends. He has many certificates nationally and internationally.

In 2006, he organised a handicap camp in Jaipur in Malviya Nagar near GT Mall. He spent a lot of money on distributing equipment to handicapped persons. At that time, an Income Tax officer troubled him and handed him an Income Tax notice. He met senior officers of the Income Tax department and explained his situation. The senior officer understood and also attended his next programme. The officer called other colleagues of his and made them understand the nature of his work and the difficulties he faces. The officer also made Jaiprakash's annual statement as zero challan. Once in 2002 in Jodhpur, Jaiprakash had an argument with the collector of Jodhpur and it got so far that the collector asked the SP to make him sit in the police station. When the handicapped people from Rajasthan came to the police station and explained the situation to the administration, everything was settled peacefully. Then the collector came by himself and patted him.

Mr. Jaiprakash has faced many difficult situations while working for the handicapped people but he keeps on working for the welfare of others. His own body doesn't function properly. His hands, legs, and spine work at only 30% capacity but still he travels all over India to help

other handicapped people without getting defeated by his own physical condition.

The story of Mr. Jaiprakash is one of grit, determination, and the spirit of never being defeated. Action is the key to success in life. His story inspires and motivates many of us.

GAYATRI CHADWA

Gayatri Chadwa

*Founder SVA Eternal,
Maharashtra State Chair, G100 Diversity &
Inclusion Wing*

Some of us are lucky to know the paths we wish to walk; others take longer to find their purpose.

This is a statement that holds true when it comes to the journey of Gayatri Chadwa, an entrepreneur, social activist, and an educator at heart.

After completing her BTech in Bioinformatics, Gayatri went into research and completed her work in stem cell research at Burns Institute in Mumbai. Education was something she enjoyed immensely and from there she began her journey as an educator. Having established an academy for private tuitions for students of various boards, she began her journey in Mumbai.

With the changing dynamics in the education system, increasing pressure and competition, she started learning more about psychology and counselling and completed a few certifications in personal counselling, student counselling and wellbeing.

Her own struggles with depression and anxiety as a teenager were the driving force to help students find stability and relaxation as they battled the academic and societal pressures to perform.

In 2014, she shifted to Pune and that's when her true journey towards the passion she had for education and mental health began.

She founded her proprietary venture, Eternal Enrichment and established the brand Sva Eternal.

Being a certified emotional intelligence and spiritual life coach, a certified Akashic records healer, a reiki and crystal reiki master, a special needs educator, an NLP practitioner and a trainee

holistic therapist, she is passionate about making a difference in the society.

Having experienced depression first-hand for many years in a row, and being unable to ask for help due to the taboo surrounding it, she struggled personally to find the way out. Though her journey has been a trying one, she is proud and content with where she is presently in her life.

Having been an educator first, teaching not just Indian students but students across the globe for more than 7 years now, the change in the way students learn has been drastic. The pressure, the demands, and the competition are at such extremes that the struggle over the years has been unfortunately too steep.

Her personal experiences and the struggles that her students faced each day, not just in the society but also within the safe spaces of home, schools, and peers were the motivation to start Sva Eternal.

Sva is 'me, myself, my own' and eternal is 'forever'. The brand name Sva Eternal came from the vision to help and facilitate people to find their own self, for their own by helping them with the right push to do so, to facilitate them to rediscover themselves, their strengths, and their powers all on their own.

The vision was to establish a safe space for all those who wish to empower themselves and be themselves, to rediscover their lost or dimmed light, a place which is all inclusive irrespective of the social strata, gender, educational backgrounds, or professional standings.

Starting something on your own is always a challenge, especially when you have a baby to look after. When she started out, she started out as a teacher, catering to students of all age groups, but seeing the struggles and the increasing pressures, she shifted her focus completely to early childhood development, mental wellbeing, and holistic healing.

And her support system of her friends and well-wishers stood by her through it all.

Over the years, since its inception, Sva has reached different heights and continues to work hard towards the betterment of the society.

Today, Gayatri has diversified in the space of inclusion and education. From individual counselling for students, women, and abuse and addiction victims to creating safe spaces for individuals with disabilities, supporting the LGBTQ+ community to conducting training sessions for educators, corporates, and students, Gayatri works full-time towards her passion of supporting individuals.

Along with being the proprietor of her own brand, she is also a partner in a newly formed organisation 'In_Sanity', which is working on promoting awareness about various social issues, by connecting with different university students and sharing their perspectives and views. The organisation aims to create a safe space for students and individuals to express themselves freely and provide mental health support at subsidiary rates to students.

She also is a part of the core team of an online platform 'The Mom Experts' that aims to help pregnant women and postpartum moms in their journeys forward.

She is a firm believer that if educators are educated and aware, they can create a stronger backbone for the future and help the blooming buds of the next generation to be more balanced in their views, more comfortable in being themselves, and more empowered from a young age. With this belief, she has trained over 3000 teachers over

the span of her work, on different topics like the mental and emotional wellbeing of teachers and students, creating inclusive classrooms, learning methodologies, and many more.

With a hope to create a network of youth who are empowered to help themselves and those around them who need support, she has trained more than 30000 students on emotional intelligence, gender identity, suicide prevention, and many other topics to help them cope with the increasing peer and societal pressures.

She has been invited as a speaker on various esteemed platforms to speak about mental wellbeing, emotional intelligence, and diversity and inclusion. Panellist at the Wellington International College Pune to talk about inclusive assessments; panellist on UN SDG 4 at SDG Symposium, Mental & Emotional Wellbeing and Building Inclusive Societies at ZocDoc, Pune; speaker at Sustainable Development Council, India; speaker at Pharmacircuit Winter Edition by Aztech Pharma; panellist and speaker at Global Workplace Wellness Summit by IWC, Canada, to speak on Workplace Wellness, DEI, and developing strategies; panellist at the Education Summit by Brainworld; Speaker

at IEEE Student Branch of Ahmedabad University are a few of her participations.

She was also a speaker on the I Speak movement by Queen Ameenata Koita and Princess Lindiwe, where she spoke about her work and inclusion. She also has in her kitty various national and international podcasts on mental health and inclusion.

After years of working with various organisations across the globe, Gayatri also works as a freelancer to help businesses in their operations and project management by sharing her expertise in the field and helps them streamline their work and organisational requirements. She also works as a consultant in various schools across Pune to help them achieve the inclusion that is needed in the society.

She was also privileged to be a speaker at the Women Economic Forum, where she was awarded the Iconic Women Building Societies award for her contribution to the society.

Along with being an entrepreneur, Gayatri believes in giving back to the society and making a difference at the grassroots level. She aims to help many different NGOs by supporting the causes and helping to bring about a difference in the society.

Gayatri holds a position in the G100 Inclusion and Diversity Wing as the State Chair for Maharashtra. She aims to create awareness and work at the grassroots level to bring about a sense of belonging for each individual.

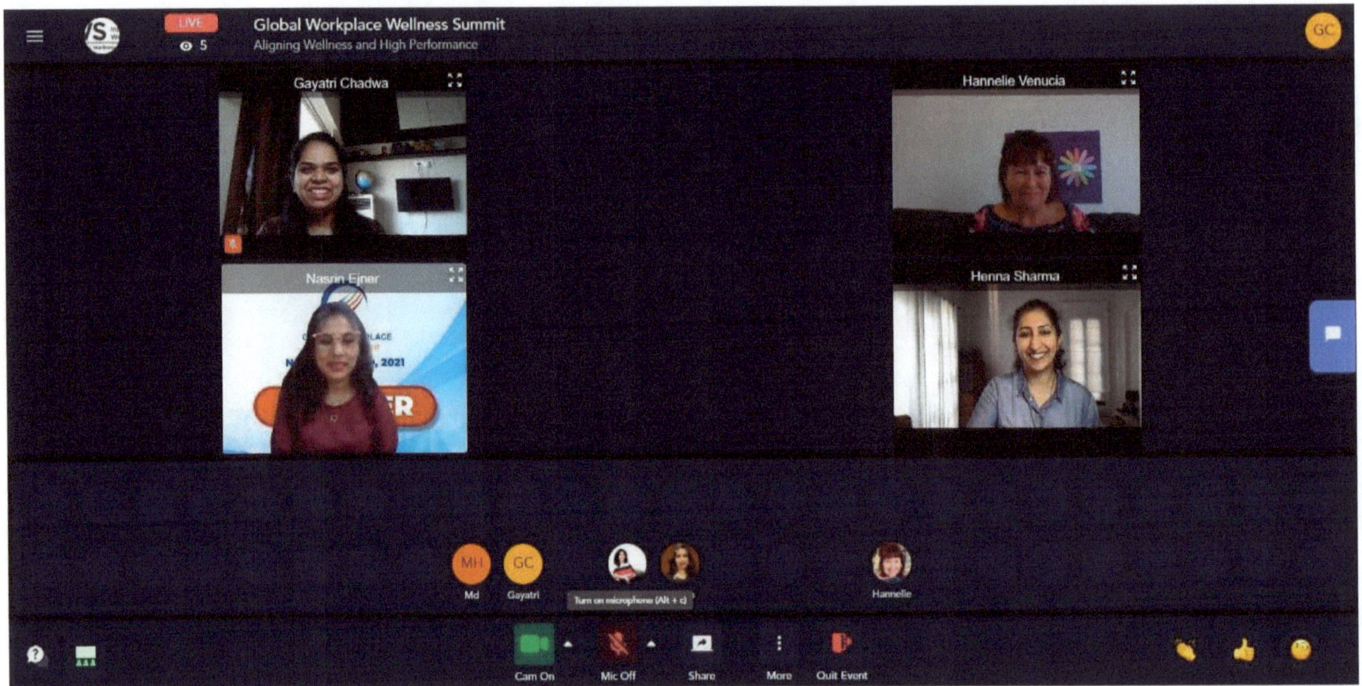
LIVE
Global Workplace Wellness Summit
Aligning Wellness and High Performance
Gayatri Chadwa
Hannelie Venucia
Nasrin Ejner
Henna Sharma
Md
Gayatri
Turn on microphone (Alt + c)
Hannelie
Cam On
Mic Off
Share
More
Quit Event

WORLD ASSOCIATION OF WOMEN WARRIORS
WORLD ASSOCIATION OF WOMEN WARRIORS
WARRIOR
INCL
#WA

Partnering with NanhaGyaan Foundation, Sva Eternal has started an initiative 'The World of Blessings', which aims at acknowledging the efforts of individuals with disabilities and creating a space for each individual with disability. Inclusion Carnival for children with developmental disabilities and Umeed Awards to felicitate any individual who has an inspirational story are the two key projects they hold under their umbrella.

Break the Silence is another initiative that she is working on along with Priya Seetharam, a psychologist based in Vancouver, Canada. They are trying to establish a council for the prevention of rape and suicide in India and spread its wings across the globe gradually. With the rise in the number of victims each day, this is one initiative very close to her heart.

She was awarded the Humanitarian Award in Education by the WAOW Foundation in March 2023. The Guru is another award she received in her span of career, the IIHM Teacher's Day award for two consecutive years and some other small recognitions for her work in the field of education and social causes.

She also holds the position of General Secretary for the BJP Education Cell, Pune and has led the creation and implementation of 'Project Drishti', which trained more than 200 teachers in a 6-month free teacher training programme. She works with different schools for the underprivileged and *basti* areas to create awareness about mental health, addictions, better education systems, self-care, and creating inclusive classrooms. She has also conducted workshops for more than 2000 teachers in the last 2 years.

Gayatri aims to help small businesses create inclusive work environments and build societies where each individual feels belonged. She wishes to help entrepreneurs address the issues that global collaborations have brought about and understand and implement strategies to help build better teams for the smooth functioning of the organisations. Her future work aims to create spaces for every individual and provide skill-based training to all. She is also working on creating efficient mental health support in underprivileged areas and helping at the grassroots level. Being a learner at heart, she continues to explore different avenues to upskill and upgrade herself in various entrepreneurial skills as well as equip herself to help the society better.

https://www.linkedin.com/in/gayatri-chadwa

NEELAM KHEMKA

Neelam Khemka

Poetess & Social Worker

"You have witnessed countless memories in the world of hearts. You are the voice of my unseen dreams. This secret buried in the depths of my heart is related to only you. You know my wishes, my desires, and my feelings."

Neelam Khemka was born into an affluent Marwari family, renowned for its rich culture, in the ancient city of Delhi. It was a time of streets, neighbourhoods, and close-knit communities. Elders were held in high regard, especially by the youth. She received her education in this environment, where teachers were regarded as equals to parents. Her educational journey started at "DAV Montessori" and continued at "Suraj Kanya Vidyalaya," eventually culminating at "Indraprastha College." After completing her bachelor's degree in the field of arts, her thirst for knowledge and inclination towards education led her to pursue a degree in journalism, along with other sporadic courses.

Neelam pursued an MA in Hindi even after getting married, despite unfavourable circumstances and lack of support. The longing

CITY BRIEFS

जेल में 200 बंदियों को दिए गए कंबल

KANPUR: जिला कारागार, कानपुर नगर में 11 जनवरी को समाज सेवी संस्था आइडियल कानपुर एसोसिएशन और ह्यूमन फाउंडेशन ने कम्बल वितरण किया. जेल अधीक्षक डॉ. बीडी पांडेय ने बताया कि संस्थाओं के सौजन्य से कुल 200 ऊनी कम्बल महिला और पुरुष बंदियों को दिए गए. इस अवसर पर संस्था से ईशांक, सुभाषिनी, नीलम खेमका, अदिति शुक्ला, रचना अवस्थी, जेलर अनिल कुमार पाण्डेय, उप कारापाल कृष्ण मोहन चन्द्र, प्रशान्त उपाध्याय, राजेश कुमार मौर्या, सॉयमा जलीस और मौसमी राय उपस्थित रहीं.

क रूप में चिकित्सा क्षेत्र में डायाबिटीज व अस्थमा रोग के उपचार में किए गए उत्कृष्ट चिकित्सा एवं शोध कार्य के लिए एपीआई प्रेजिडेंट व अंतरराष्ट्रीय स्तर पर सम्मानित किया जा चुका है। डॉ राहुल का यह सम्मान मिलने पर देश के विभिन्न राज्यों से बधाई संदेश मिल रहे हैं।

गणतंत्र दिवस पर और बसंत पंचमी की शाम को जिया साहित्य मंच पर पर एक सुंदर काव्य संगोष्ठी का आयोजन

नई दिल्ली ■ हम हिंदुस्तानी

गणतंत्र दिवस पर और बसंत पंचमी पर 26 जनवरी की शाम को जिया साहित्य मंच पर पर ऑनलाइन राष्ट्रीय काव्य संगोष्ठी का आयोजन हुआ। 26 जनवरी को परम पूज्य जिया माँ (रामाश्रम सत्संग) जन्म जयंती पर भजन जयपुर से भजन गायिका व रामाश्रम सत्संगी संतोष पारीक ने जिया माँ के चरणों में अपने भाव पूर्ण भजन से श्रद्धा सुमन अर्पित किए। उसके बाद ओटावा कनाडा से रश्मि सिन्हा ने जिया माँ के चरणों में अपनी सुंदर कविता अर्पित की। अयोध्या से मनोरमा मिश्रा ने काव्य गोष्ठी का शुभारंभ सरस्वती वंदना से किया। सबसे पहले बेंगलुरु से रीता सिंह ने स्वागत उद्बोधन दिया।

इस काव्य गोष्ठी में गोष्ठी में भारत के साथ- साथ विदेशों से भी प्रसिद्ध कविगण जुड़े थे। मुख्य अतिथि के रूप में मुख्य वरिष्ठ साहित्यकार प्रकाशक संपादक व पत्रकार मोहन शर्मा ने अपनी उपस्थिति से काव्य गोष्ठी की गरिमा बढ़ाई। 2 दर्जन से अधिक सम्मान पत्रों से सम्मानित मनमोहन शर्मा 'शरण' जी को (वर्ष 2009), में दिल्ली की तत्कालीन मुख्यमंत्री श्रीमती 'शीला दीक्षित' जी से नैतिक सम्मान प्राप्त हुआ था। ब्रिटेन के तत्कालीन प्रधान मंत्री श्री टोनी ब्लेयर जी से प्रशंसा पत्र प्राप्त कर चुके हैं। वर्ष 2019 में परम पूज्य संत मोरारी बापू जी से 'उत्कर्ष मेल' तथा अनुराधा प्रकाशन की एक पुस्तक का लोकार्पण जिसका आस्था चैनल पर लाइव प्रसारण हुआ था, इसी पुस्तक का लोकार्पण सम्मान में भारत के राष्ट्रपति महामहिम श्री राम नाथ कोविंद जी से मिलना हुआ, अभी हाल ही में 23 फरवरी 2021 को भारत की वित्तमंत्री श्रीमती निर्मला सीतारमण जी से भेंट हुई, उन्होंने उत्कर्ष मेल तथा अनुराधा प्रकाशन की 2 पुस्तकों को अपना आशीर्वाद दिया तथा लोकार्पित किया। आपने एक शॉर्ट फिल्म 'आरक्षण की बलि' का भी निर्माण किया। 28 जून को स्वाइस रेडियो कनाडा में मनमोहन शर्मा 'शरण' का योग दिवस पर साक्षात्कार प्रसारित हुआ। मंडी हाउस में हुए नाटक 'ये मौत क्यों रात भर नहीं आती' में विशिष्ट अतिथि के रूप में भागीदारी, इसके अतिरिक्त अनेक नाटकों के आयोजन अथवा साहित्यिक आयोजनों में मुख्य अतिथि तथा विशिष्ट अतिथि के रूप में भागीदारी। पत्रकारिता में उल्लेखनीय योगदान के निमित्त चेन्नई में आयोजित विशाल दीक्षांत समारोह में मानद डॉक्टरेट की उपाधि से सम्मानित हो चुके हैं। मनमोहन शर्मा ने जिया साहित्य मंच की शान में अपनी शानदार पंक्तियां व सुंदर काव्य पाठ भी प्रस्तुत किया। कानपुर से कवित्री नीलम खेमका ने सैनिकों को समर्पित एक सुंदर कविता प्रस्तुत की। सोनीपत हरियाणा से राजश्री गौड़, कतर दोहा से एम डी एस रामालक्ष्मी, जौनपुर से सागर सिंह, बड़ौदी गुजरात से गिरिजा गुप्ता, दिल्ली से राजेश श्रीवास्तव, शिमला हिमाचल प्रदेश से पवन भारद्वाज, औरैया से रचना शर्मा, मुंबई से चंद्रमोहन नीले, बेंगलुरु कर्नाटका से उषा कंसल, बेंगलुरु से ही अजिता सरन आदि सभी कवि व कवयित्रियों ने भारत देश व बसंत पंचमी पर सुंदर रचनाएं प्रस्तुत की। बेंगलुरु से रीता सिंह ने काव्य गोष्ठी का संचालन किया सैनिकों को समर्पित एक मार्मिक कविता प्रस्तुत की। अयोध्या से मनोरमा मिश्रा ने सभी कवियों की कविताओं को ध्यान से सुन कर उनकी सुंदर समीक्षा की व देश के ऊपर एक सुंदर कविता प्रस्तुत की।

बीते बुधवार, 11 जनवरी, 2023 को आइडियल कानपुर एसोसिएशन के प्रोजेक्ट में **Humane Foundation** ने भी सहयोग किया। कानपुर जेल में 200 कम्बल वितरित हुए। इसमें मुख्य रूप से एफ. डी. अली, रचना अवस्थी, नीलम खेमका, इशांक का सहयोग रहा। **Humane Foundation** की संस्थापक श्रीमती अदिति शुक्ला ने बताया कि अगले एक हफ्ते में **Humane Foundation** ने वहाँ 1000 कम्बल पहुँचाने का संकल्प किया है।   – दैनिक कानपुर उजाला

to continue learning and progressing kept her restless for years. The frustration of being unable to fully utilise her abilities haunted her. During this time, with the encouragement of her elder sister, she joined the "Jessie's Club." Notably, her sister covered her membership fee. It was at this club that her creative talents flourished. She eventually became the president of the club and held the unopposed position of "Jessie's International Wing Chairman" for four years. She excelled in stage management and was highly regarded for her disciplined approach to administration.

With two children, Neelam still had many paths to explore. Separation from family, her husband's prolonged illness, financial crises, and concerns about her children's future could have broken any woman, wife, or mother mentally and physically. She was no exception. She faced numerous surgeries and managed financial crises by offering courses and projects to school children.

Amidst these challenging days, Neelam enrolled in a Reiki course. Sahchar's efforts granted her the joy of "her terrace," and she continued her artistic pursuits in Tanjore painting and ceramic pottery. She carried on with her artistic endeavours, but the desire to learn music remained dormant in the corners of her mind. In the midst of all this, she began writing poems and Sher O Shayari (couplets) due to the artistic legacy inherited from her father. Her passion for education led her to courses in body language, tarot reading, colour therapy, dream analysis, landscaping, gardening, and interior decoration. She embraced the path of social work,

guided by the ethos of "Apna Haath Jagannath," which signifies taking matters into one's own hands. She attended programs as a "special guest," and established her identity as a social worker and writer. Her first song was produced by "Thirak" Music. She then sang "Manuhar Geet" in her own voice and produced "Tanak Hari" with "T-Series." In 2019, she had the privilege of having Sadhna Sargam ji sing her self-written production "Ganga Aarti." Throughout this journey, she published five books, and in the fifth book, all the paintings are her own creations.

If not for physical limitations and proper guidance, Neelam might have left her mark even in the sky through painting. Still, with four years of experience at "Factory Point" and three years of running a boutique, coupled with her role as a Bureau Chief in a newspaper, she acquired skills in motivational speaking, time management, and giving grooming tips. There is no age limit for learning in this journey of life. She learns whenever she desires, and remembers that the true essence of

life lies in "live and let live" – simply love without expecting anything in return.